ACTS BIBLE STUDY

DISCOVER HOW THE EARLY CHURCH CAN INFORM WHAT WE DO TODAY

40-DAY BIBLE STUDY SERIES
BOOK 2

PETER DEHAAN

Acts Bible Study: Discover How the Early Church Can Inform What We Do Today

Library of Congress Control Number: 2025904521

Published by Rock Rooster Books

ISBN:

- 979-8-88809-134-0 (e-book)
- 979-8-88809-135-7 (paperback)
- 979-8-88809-136-4 (hardcover)
- 979-8-88809-137-1 (audiobook)

Credits:

- Developmental editor: Cathy Rueter
- Copyeditor: Robyn Mulder
- Cover design: Fanderclai Design
- Author photo: Chelsie Jensen Photography

To Christopher Alexander

Series by Peter DeHaan

40-Day Bible Study Series takes a fresh and practical look into Scripture, book by book.

Bible Character Sketches Series celebrates people in Scripture, from the well-known to the obscure.

Holiday Celebration Bible Study Series rejoices in the holidays with Jesus.

Visiting Churches Series takes an in-person look at church practices and traditions to inform and inspire today's followers of Jesus.

Be the first to hear about Peter's new books and receive updates at PeterDeHaan.com/updates.

CONTENTS

WHO IS LUKE?

Paul is the most prolific writer in the New Testament. Who's second? Doctor Luke.

Luke wrote a biography of Jesus, called "The Gospel According to Luke" (or simply *Luke*). Later, he detailed the activities of the early church in a sequel, "The Acts of the Apostles" (or just *Acts*). These two books account for about one-quarter of the content in the Bible's New Testament and give us valuable historical information about Jesus and his followers. Luke's writings provide a compelling two-book set that can inform our faith and enlighten the practices of our church community.

Luke is the only non-Jewish writer in the New Testament. As such, his words are that of an outsider, which may more readily connect with those on the outside, that is, non-Jews. This includes me, and it may include you. Luke wrote with simple, yet captivating language.

However, despite having penned two major books in the Bible—which are the longest two in the New Testament—we don't know much about Luke. The Bible only mentions him three times.

Here are the few details we know:

First, we learn that Luke is a *dear friend* of Paul. Next, he's a *doctor*. Third, he's esteemed by Paul as a *fellow worker*. Finally, in one of his darker hours, Paul laments that everyone is gone. Only Luke has stayed with him. As such, we see Luke as a faithful, persevering friend. Luke emerges as a man of noble character.

We also know that Luke is a firsthand observer in many of the events he records in the book of Acts. We see this through his first-person narratives in some passages when he uses the pronoun *we*.

Although Luke wasn't a church leader or an apostle, his contributions to our faith and our understanding of Jesus and his church are significant. Doctor Luke's ministry function wasn't leading people or preaching sermons. Instead, he played a silent, and almost unnoticed, supporting role.

Though his work was quiet, his legacy lives on, loudly influencing Jesus's followers two millennia later.

What can we do to influence others for Jesus, both now and in the future?

[Discover more about Luke in Colossians 4:14, 2 Timothy 4:9–11, and Philemon 1:24.]

ALL ABOUT ACTS

Acts is one of the sixty-six books in the Protestant Bible. It details the actions ("the Acts") of Jesus's band of followers. As such, Acts supplies a compelling narrative of life in the early church as it emerges after Jesus's execution.

Authored by Doctor Luke, Acts records the work of Jesus's followers as they navigate unmapped territory. It forms a new faith perspective based on the teachings of Jesus and the supporting work of the Holy Spirit. Luke gives a valuable narrative to inform us and to reform our church practices. As a Gentile, Luke is also an outsider to Judaism—just like most of us.

As the narrative in Acts progresses, we see Luke

sometimes shifting from a third-person perspective, that of a reporter, to a first-person point of view as a participant. Though the good doctor writes his first book, Luke, as an outsider, he emerges in his second book, Acts, as an insider, where he takes part in the work of Paul to develop Jesus's church.

Clearly Luke, the former reporter, has become a follower of Jesus and part of his growing community of believers. This book explores what Luke shares in his informative description about the early church in the book of Acts, which can teach us much about faith and inform our church practice.

Each of Luke's two books, Luke and Acts, address Theophilus.

We don't know who Theophilus is, only that Luke writes both of his books to Theophilus so that he may know for sure what others had taught him about Jesus.

Luke has two notable traits to make him ideal for this task. First, as a doctor, he's a trained observer. This makes him an ideal investigative reporter for Theophilus.

Second, as a non-Jew, Luke has a fresh take on the subject, without historical baggage to distract him on his mission.

This helps Theophilus, and it helps us.

What steps are we willing to take to help someone, like Theophilus, know for certain what they were taught?

[Discover more about Theophilus in Luke 1:1–4 and Acts 1:1–2.]

DAY 1: WAIT FOR IT
ACTS 1:1–8

"Do not leave Jerusalem, but wait for the gift my Father promised, which you have heard me speak about." (Acts 1:4)

A cts picks up where the book of Luke ended. As with many sequels, Acts opens with a review of what happened in the first book. Again addressing Theophilus, Luke references his first letter, which we call Luke, the third book in the New Testament.

Here's the recap: In the forty days between Jesus's resurrection and his return to heaven, he appears to his followers many times. He proves he's alive and reminds them about the kingdom of God. Slowly, things begin to click for them. Jesus isn't a military leader who will overthrow the Roman rule. He's a spiritual revolutionary to fulfill God's plan for humanity, set in motion before time began.

Finally, Jesus's teaching starts to take on new meaning. The misconceptions of his followers' prior thinking fall away. But it takes time to reorient their perspective from the physical world to a spiritual reality. When one of his followers asks if Jesus is ready to restore Israel as a nation, his answer is "not now." The timing is secret.

Instead, Jesus tells his followers to wait.

Waiting is counter to our modern-day thinking. Delay represents lost opportunity. We must maintain momentum to propel our cause forward. Yet Jesus says, "Wait." It seems ill-advised. However, much of what Jesus says is contrary to human wisdom. We should expect the unexpected from Jesus. If he says to wait, this shouldn't cause dismay. Sometimes inaction is the best action—especially when God says to delay.

From a human perspective, they should organize, plan, and deploy across the region to tell others about Jesus. They have experience going out two-by-two. Jesus trained them to do just that. They seem ready, but Jesus says to wait.

Wait for a special gift promised by Papa: a new

kind of baptism, a supernatural anointing. While John uses water, this new baptism will be with the Holy Spirit. The Holy Spirit will empower them to tell others about Jesus.

This new baptism doesn't have the tangible use of water but the intangible power of Spirit. Yet the two are connected, for the Holy Spirit shows up when John baptizes Jesus with water.

Consider John's baptism. He lowers people into the water, submerges them, and lifts them out. John's baptism symbolically parallels death, burial, and resurrection. Cleansing takes place. It's a powerful, beautiful imagery.

When Jesus emerges from the waters of his baptism, heaven opens and the Holy Spirit, in a visible form that resembles a dove, comes upon him. God's voice booms. He confirms Jesus as his son, whom he loves and whose actions he affirms. In this case, Jesus's water baptism links to the Holy Spirit. This foreshadows what is to come for his disciples with the promised gift of the Holy Spirit.

While different streams of Christianity explain the Holy Spirit's work in different ways, with varying present-day implications, we should use what happened then to inform our understanding and practices now.

Do we need to reconsider the role of the Holy Spirit in our life and our church to better align with the Bible?

[Discover more about the Holy Spirit in Acts 2:38, Acts 10:44–45, Acts 11:15–16, Acts 19:2–6, Romans 15:13, 1 Corinthians 6:19, and Jude 1:20–21.]

DAY 2: THERE'S NO NEED TO VOTE
ACTS 1:9–26

So they nominated two men: Joseph called Barsabbas (also known as Justus) and Matthias. (Acts 1:23)

After Jesus tells his followers to wait for the Holy Spirit, he rises into heaven. Though Jesus tells them to wait, he doesn't say to do nothing.

They spend their time in constant prayer. This could mean nonstop, around-the-clock prayer or just that they prayed a lot. Regardless, I suspect they prayed much more than we ever do.

Their numbers grow, reaching 120. Peter speaks. He reviews what happened, ties in Old

Testament prophecy, and quotes Psalm 109:8. He recommends they pick a replacement for Judas.

Peter gives one requirement: it must be someone who followed Jesus the whole time, from his baptism to his ascension, a person who can confirm Jesus's resurrection. Peter gives no other credentials. A connection with Jesus stands as the only require- ment. Education, social status, and reputation aren't a consideration. Power, money, and influence don't matter. We might want to consider this as we pick our church leaders.

In most churches today, we would nominate and then vote. This democratic solution is what most modern thinkers hold up as the ideal approach. Yet the Bible does nothing to promote democratic rule. Yes, if we search God's Word looking to support democracy, we can find hints of it. However, looking through different lenses we could also conclude the Bible points toward socialism, commu- nism, or even dictatorships. Yet the early church often relies on consensus. But theocracy, under God's Holy Spirit authority, might be the ideal biblical conclusion for government.

Following Peter's advice to pick someone who walked with Jesus, the group nominates two men: Barsabbas and Matthias. Then the brothers and sisters pray. They acknowledge that God knows everyone's heart, including the two nominees. The church affirms God has already chosen Judas's replacement, and they simply ask God to reveal his decision. Then they cast lots. They do so, confident that God will let the results fall to the person he wants in this role. The church accepts the outcome in complete faith.

While we may equate this to drawing names from a hat, a better understanding is akin to throwing dice. This seems most undignified, even a bit pagan. Yet picking the next disciple resembles a game of chance, albeit with a God-orchestrated outcome. The lot falls to Matthias. He replaces Judas to become the twelfth disciple and an apostolic minister.

Though the church casts lots in this instance to select a leader, we must note that Luke merely describes their process. It's not a command. We may follow this model or not.

In all this I feel sorry for Barsabbas. It isn't that he loses a human election. Instead God decides, and he dismisses Barsabbas. If he wallows in self-pity, he could conclude that God rejected him. Barsabbas could stomp off in anger and leave the church, embarrassed over the Almighty not picking him. As a testament to his character, he doesn't leave in a huff. He sticks around and becomes an esteemed leader. Later the church taps him for an important assignment with Paul, Barnabas, and Silas.

Interestingly, we never hear of Matthias again in the Bible.

While Barsabbas rose above his disappointment, could it be that Matthias squandered his God-given opportunity? What can we learn from their examples?

[Discover more about casting lots in Joshua 18:10, Judges 20:9, Nehemiah 10:34, and Jonah 1:7, as well as Luke 23:34.]

DIG DEEPER: WHY TWELVE?

When evening came, Jesus arrived with the Twelve. (Mark 14:17)

Jesus had twelve disciples. Twelve is significant. Recall that Jacob had twelve sons. They became the twelve tribes of Israel, God's chosen people.

And Jesus selected twelve disciples to head up his followers, who become his chosen people, the elect.

Having twelve disciples maintains a symbolic connection between God the Father's people of the Old Testament with God the Son's people in the New Testament. (Interestingly, Abraham's other son, Ishmael, also had twelve sons, which became twelve tribes too. That's worth keeping in mind.)

When Judas commits suicide, it just won't do to leave them with eleven disciples. To keep the symbolic connection to the Old Testament, they must replace Judas, restoring the numeric imagery.

Twelve appears in other places in the Bible too —about 130 times. In the writings of Moses, there are twelve stones, twelve loaves, twelve silver plates, twelve silver sprinkling bowls, and twelve gold dishes, along with many more mentions of twelve. A lot of these twelves relate to worship.

In Revelation, there are twelve stars, twelve gates and twelve angels, twelve foundations, twelve pearls, and twelve crops of fruit. John's vision reinforces the number twelve, as well.

Is this a hint that there's a connection between the past (twelve tribes), the present (twelve disciples), and the future (twelve of many things)?

What do you think about the recurring mentions of twelve in the Bible?

[Discover more about Jesus's twelve disciples in Matthew 10:1–4. Discover more about the number twelve in Genesis 25:13–16, Exodus 28:21, Exodus 39:14, Leviticus 24:5, Numbers 7:84, Revelation 12:1, Revelation 21:12, 14, & 21, and Revelation 22:2.]

DAY 3: THE GIFT OF THE HOLY SPIRIT
ACTS 2:1–41

*When they heard this sound, a crowd came together in
bewilderment, because each one heard their own language
being spoken.* (Acts 2:6)

Just before Jesus returns to heaven, he tells
his disciples to wait in Jerusalem for a
present that Papa will send: the gift of Holy
Spirit power. Then Jesus ascends, returning
to his heavenly father. The disciples go back to
Jerusalem to wait as commanded. As they wait, they
select a replacement for Judas, and they do a lot of
praying.

Ten days later Pentecost happens.

Nothing like this has ever occurred before. Yet there are hints of it in both the Old and New Testaments. In Exodus, the people wait at the bottom of a mountain. There's thunder, lightning, and a deafening trumpet blast. The people tremble. Smoke covers the mountain. There's fire, and there's more smoke. The earth quakes. God appears.

In the New Testament, after John baptizes Jesus, the Holy Spirit—looking like a dove—comes upon Jesus. Then the booming voice of Father God affirms his son.

Later, at a supernatural event we call the Transfiguration, Jesus takes Peter, John, and James up a mountain. Jesus's face glows like the sun and his clothes dazzle a bright white. Suddenly Moses and Elijah show up and the three have a conversation. Again, Father God speaks, "I love my boy and want you to listen to him."

Each of these three stories parallels what's about to happen at Pentecost. They're all connected.

At Pentecost, Father God's gift does indeed arrive. The sound of rushing wind fills the place. Something that looks like flames of fire rests on each person. The Holy Spirit fills them, and they speak in other languages.

Perplexed, a crowd gathers. Each person hears the disciples speaking in their own language. The people freak out, trying to fathom what this all means. But others mock the disciples, thinking they're drunk.

It's only been fifty days since Jesus overcame death by rising from the dead, and it's only been ten days since he returned to heaven. Prior to that, Jesus spent his public ministry teaching about the kingdom of God and preparing his disciples to continue without him—at least without him in person.

Yet they need the Holy Spirit to fully equip them for ministry. They can't go forward on their own and hope to succeed. That's why Jesus told them to wait for Holy Spirit power.

Now, supernaturally empowered, Peter speaks boldly. Three thousand people believe in Jesus and are baptized. And this is just the beginning of what the Holy Spirit enables Jesus's followers to do. The Holy Spirit will change everything.

Seeing what the Holy Spirit can do should inspire and energize us with endless possibilities.

Do we need to wait for the Holy Spirit? How can we move under Holy Spirit power?

[Discover more about God's power in Exodus 19:16–20, Matthew 17:5, and Luke 3:22.]

DAY 4: A BIBLICAL MODEL FOR CHURCH

ACTS 2:42–47

And the Lord added to their number daily those who were being saved. (Acts 2:47)

After Jesus's followers receive Papa's gift of the Holy Spirit at Pentecost, Luke describes what happens next. It's huge.

First, they dedicate themselves to learning more about Jesus from his disciples. They do this in community, not isolation. Luke uses the word fellowship.

Next, they eat meals together. Luke calls this breaking bread. They do this in their homes. Again, more community.

Third, they focus on prayer.

These three traits form the basis for what happens next. As they learn about Jesus, form community, and pray, other things unfold.

One action, which may seem quite foreign to us today, is that they share everything they have with those in need. Interestingly, this generosity is with those within Jesus's church, not those outside it. They even sell their property and donate the proceeds for the common good of their group.

Another thing they do is meet daily. This is in the temple. They meet in public, too, perhaps so more people can join Team Jesus.

As they do this, they persist in eating together at people's homes, in gladness and with sincerity.

Last, they praise God.

As the result of all this, they earn the respect of everyone. Did you get that? Everyone.

What's the outcome?

More people join them. How amazing is that?

Let's recap. Here are the seven things the early church does:

1. They learn more about Jesus from those who know him better.

2. They eat meals together.
3. They spend a lot of time praying.
4. They share what they have with each other, so that no one is in need.
5. They meet daily in public.
6. They enjoy meals together in each other's homes, in celebration.
7. They praise God.

We could turn this into a model for how Jesus's followers should behave. Though we wouldn't be wrong in following this example of the early church, we must remember that this is not a command of how to operate. It's merely a description of what the church did. However, since the outcome is more people following Jesus, we see that God blesses what they did.

In looking at the behavior of the early church, we see that they did everything as a group. No one pursued their faith in isolation. They functioned in community. In fact, there's a hint that they functioned in complete unity. Luke writes that *all* Jesus's followers hung out together, not just some of them, but all. There weren't distinct groups, factions, or locations. They were one, just as Jesus and his

Father are one, which is what Jesus prayed for before he died.

What can today's church learn from this description of the early church?

[Discover more about Jesus's passion for unity in John 17:20–21.]

DIG DEEPER: LET'S BREAK BREAD

They devoted themselves to the apostles' teaching and to fellowship, to the breaking of bread and to prayer. (Acts 2:42)

We read about breaking bread in the Bible. Interestingly, this is a New Testament reference. It doesn't appear in the Old Testament. We first encounter this concept when Jesus turns the Passover celebration into the Lord's Supper, which establishes Communion or the Eucharist.

In his Passover celebration with his disciples, Jesus picks up a loaf of bread, breaks it into pieces, and passes it around the table. Hence, he broke bread. We could, therefore, conclude that *breaking bread* is a reference to Communion.

Yes, but it's more than that.

A broader understanding is that breaking bread is a euphemism for sharing a meal with other followers of Jesus. In the most generic sense, breaking bread covers any meal we eat with others.

As we break bread with other followers of Jesus, there's a sense of shared community, of fellowship as part of Jesus's family. When we break bread, we eat with intention, keeping Jesus at the center of our food celebration. And a special type of breaking bread is the one when we celebrate Communion.

How often do we break bread with others in spiritual, Jesus-centered community?

[Discover more about breaking bread in Luke 24:30, Acts 20:7, and Acts 20:11. Read about Holy Communion in Matthew 26:26–29, Mark 14:22–25, Luke 22:19–23, and 1 Corinthians 11:23–29.]

DAY 5: PETER HEALS A DISABLED MAN

ACTS 3:1 TO ACTS 4:4

Then Peter said, "Silver or gold I do not have, but what I do have I give you. In the name of Jesus Christ of Nazareth, walk." (Acts 3:6)

One afternoon, Peter and John head to the temple to pray. As they approach the gate of the temple courtyard, they meet a man who can't walk—he never could. Every day friends carry him to the temple entrance so he can beg from the people as they head in to worship. He does this every day.

As the two disciples are about to enter, the lame man asks for money. Peter and John can ignore him and walk past. Or, if they feel generous, they can toss a couple coins his way. But they don't do either of these things.

Instead Peter says to the man, "Look at us!" The man does, expecting a nice handout. "We're broke, but what I do have, I give to you. In the name of Jesus get up and walk." Peter takes the man by his hand and helps him stand—for the first time in his life. Instantly the man's feet and ankles grow strong. He jumps. He walks. Leaping and praising God, he enters the temple courtyard to worship.

How amazing.

God's Holy Spirit power is at work, allowing a man who has never walked to do so for the first time.

This creates a stir among the people and gets their attention. Performing a miracle opens them to hear what Peter has to say. He tells them about Jesus. As he speaks, the religious leaders (who don't like what happened), along with the captain of the temple guard come up to Peter and John. They arrest the two disciples and throw them in jail.

But because of Peter's bold message, many more people believe in Jesus—up to two thousand more—swelling their number to about five thousand.

This miracle gathered an audience who was open to hear about Jesus. Holy Spirit power at work proceeds people's decisions to follow Jesus.

But let's not rush past the miracle.

The man didn't ask to walk. He asked for money.

In his focus to reach the temple for prayer—a most spiritual activity—Peter could have thrown a couple bucks at the man and gone into the temple to worship God with a clear conscience, knowing that he helped a poor man.

Giving the man money would've helped him for a day or two. But healing him will help him for the rest of his life.

Peter ignored giving the man what he wanted and instead gave him what he needed. This is a lesson for us when it comes to helping people in need.

What is our response when people ask us for money? Do we ignore them, give them what they want, or supply what they truly need?

[Discover more about helping others in Luke 6:27–36.]

DAY 6: WHO SHOULD WE OBEY?

ACTS 4:5–22

"But to stop this thing from spreading any further among the people, we must warn them to speak no longer to anyone in this name." (Acts 4:17)

After healing the lame man and forever changing his life, Peter and John spend the night in jail for their good deed. The next day they're dragged before the religious leaders to defend their actions. Will they be released for doing something good or punished for upsetting the religious leaders who can't see God at work? Will these people who killed Jesus also try to kill Peter and John? It's possible.

The man they healed is at the hearing too. He spends the first day of his life as an abled-bodied man in court. Instead of celebrating his good fortune of being healed, he's worried what the religious leaders might do to him because of it.

To begin their inquiry, the Jewish bosses demand that the two disciples explain themselves. "Under what power or whose authority did you heal this man?"

Filled with the Holy Spirit, Peter launches into a sermon. His court testimony becomes a faith testimony to all who sit there, pointing them to the saving power of Jesus.

Peter first reminds them that what he did— healing a man who couldn't walk—is a good thing. Then he boldly affirms that he did so in the name of Jesus—who, by the way, the religious leaders killed. Because of Jesus, this once lame man, who now *stands* before them, can walk. "Jesus is the cornerstone," Peter says, "and only through him can anyone be saved."

Peter, along with John, speaks with courage. Seeing how these unschooled commoners testify with such power astonishes the religious leaders. They realize these disciples had spent time with

Jesus, suggesting their power did, in fact, come from him.

The religious council, the Sanhedrin, discusses what to do. With the formerly disabled man standing before them, they can't deny that the miracle took place, but they want to squelch this growing movement before it spreads any more. They give Peter and John a strict warning—a command—to not speak of Jesus again or teach anyone about him.

Peter and John don't say "yes," and they don't say "no." Instead they ask a question: "Should we obey you or God? Think about it. As for us, we must tell others about Jesus."

The Council threatens them further, but in the end, they let Peter and John go. They can't risk punishing the disciples, because everyone is praising God for the miracle that took place.

Being so focused on their religious institution and manmade traditions, the religious leaders are unable—or unwilling—to see God at work. May we never be like them.

How do we react when the new thing God is doing differs from what he once did? Do we fight the change or embrace it?

[Discover more about God doing a new thing in Isaiah 43:19.]

DIG DEEPER: THE OLD TESTAMENT QUOTED IN ACTS

All Scripture is God-breathed and is useful for teaching,
rebuking, correcting and training in righteousness.
(2 Timothy 3:16)

T he book of Acts has twenty-nine references to passages in the Old Testament Scriptures. It quotes eight books in all, with the top three being Psalms (nine times), Exodus (six), and Isaiah (five).

Most of these appear in the various sermons recorded in Acts, by Peter, Stephen, and Paul. In the only message given by Stephen, he quotes from ten passages.

Here are all twenty-nine Old Testament citations found in the book of Acts.

1. Acts 1:20 quotes from Psalm 69:25.
2. Acts 1:20 also quotes from Psalm 109:8.
3. Acts 2:17–21 quotes from Joel 2:28–32.
4. Acts 2:28 quotes from Psalm 16:11.
5. Acts 2:31 quotes from Psalm 16:10.
6. Acts 2:34–35 quotes from Psalm 110:1.
7. Acts 3:22–23 quotes from Deuteronomy 18:15, 18–19.
8. Acts 3:25 quotes from Genesis 22:18 and Genesis 26:4.
9. Acts 4:11 quotes from Psalm 118:22.
10. Acts 4:25–26 quotes from Psalm 2:1–2.
11. Acts 7:3 quotes from Genesis 12:1.
12. Acts 7:6–7 quotes from Genesis 15:13–14.
13. Acts 7:18 quotes from Exodus 1:8.
14. Acts 7:27–28 quotes from Exodus 2:14.
15. Acts 7:32 quotes from Exodus 3:6.
16. Acts 7:33–34 quotes from Exodus 3:5–10.
17. Acts 7:37 quotes from Deuteronomy 18:15.

18. Acts 7:40 quotes from Exodus 32:1 and 23.
19. Acts 7:42–43 quotes from Amos 5:25–27.
20. Acts 7:49–50 quotes from Isaiah 66:1–2.
21. Acts 8:32–33 quotes from Isaiah 53:7–8.
22. Acts 13:33 quotes from Psalm 2:7.
23. Acts 13:34 quotes from Isaiah 55:3.
24. Acts 13:35 quotes from Psalm 16:10.
25. Acts 13:41 quotes from Habakkuk 1:5.
26. Acts 13:47 quotes from Isaiah 49:6.
27. Acts 15:16–17 quotes from Amos 9:11–12.
28. Acts 23:5 quotes from Exodus 22:28.
29. Acts 28:26–27 quotes from Isaiah 6:9–10.

It's unlikely the disciples, who quoted these passages, had a scroll to refer to, and they certainly didn't have the internet to use for research. Instead they had these passages memorized and could recall them as needed to make their points.

How many of these references do you know? Have you memorized any of them? Let's celebrate each one. As Paul wrote to Timothy, all Scripture is useful to us. So we will do well to know it and memorize it.

If we only had our memory to go by, how many verses would we know?

[Discover more about memorizing Scripture in Psalm 119:11.]

DAY 7: A PRAYER FOR BOLDNESS AND POWER

ACTS 4:23–31

After they prayed, the place where they were meeting was shaken. And they were all filled with the Holy Spirit and spoke the word of God boldly. (Acts 4:31)

I f they didn't already know it, Peter and John now realize that following Jesus can have consequences. They have done the right thing, for the right reasons, in healing the man who couldn't walk. But they're in trouble with the religious elite. They face punishment, even execution. This time they avoid both. This time the religious council releases them unharmed. Though they spent the night in jail, they're now free to leave.

They go straight to their people, who are

worried about the fate of their leaders. Though Luke doesn't mention this, I envision a massive prayer meeting, urgently interceding for the safe release of Peter and John.

The freed disciples tell everyone what happened at the religious council. They relate what the Jewish leaders said to them, warning them to never speak of Jesus again, before releasing them. This report encourages everyone. They respond by praising God in prayer, even quoting part of a Psalm.

Had it been me, I would have wrapped up my prayer thanking God for my safety and asking him for protection from my enemies. Fortunately, the early church doesn't think the way I do. Their faith is stronger, and their kingdom vision is greater.

Considering the threats of the religious leaders and seeing the future risks of telling others about Jesus, they don't ask for safety or protection. They ask for power to speak with even greater boldness. Knowing that healing people in Jesus's name gives them a platform to tell others about him, they ask God to empower them to heal and perform more miracles.

When they finish praying, the building they're meeting in shakes, just like at Pentecost. The Holy Spirit fills everyone present, just like at Pentecost.

They speak about God with great boldness, just like at Pentecost.

In this way, God affirms their heart's desire to perform supernatural signs, heal others in Jesus's name, and tell people about him with boldness. They're ready and willing to suffer to advance the cause of Jesus.

How much are we willing to suffer for following Jesus?

[Discover more about suffering for Jesus in John 21:18–19, 2 Corinthians 11:24–27, and 1 Peter 3:14–17.]

DIG DEEPER: MIRACLES, SIGNS, AND WONDERS

"Stretch out your hand to heal and perform signs and wonders through the name of your holy servant Jesus." (Acts 4:30)

In the book of Acts, we see repeated mentions of miracles, signs, and wonders. We read of Team Jesus healing people and casting out evil spirits (performing exorcisms). Why don't we experience this same Holy Spirit power today?

Some people do. In many parts of the world, the supernatural is common. It's the norm, while for other areas, it's the exception.

Some who don't see the Holy Spirit at work in their life attempt to explain it away, claiming that supernatural power died with the disciples. Yet there is no biblical support for this. These people build their theology around their experiences, not the Word of God. We should start with the Bible as the foundation for our theology. If our experiences don't align with the biblical account, what should we do to reconcile the two?

If we want to experience the supernatural power of Jesus and the Holy Spirit—the way the early church did—we need to pray for it, just like they did. Then we need to move forward in faith that miracles, signs, and wonders can still happen today.

How can the book of Acts inform our embrace of Holy Spirit power and moving in the supernatural today?

[Discover more about performing miracles in Matthew 13:58, Mark 6:5–6, Acts 3:16, and Acts 14:9–10.]

DAY 8: DON'T BE A POSER

ACTS 4:32 TO ACTS 5:11

Peter said to her, "How could you conspire to test the Spirit of the Lord?" (Acts 5:9)

In Acts 2:42–47, we read about a biblical model for church. Remember that this is a description of what happened and not a command for what to do, yet it can still guide us in our pursuit of spiritual community today. Acts chapter 4 wraps up with another description of what the early church did. We will do well to figure out how to apply this today too.

The church is united. They all get along. Luke writes that they have a singular focus. They don't claim ownership of anything, but instead they share what they have with the other believers. As a result of their unity, focus, and willingness to share, the church of Jesus moves forward with great power, and they tell others about Jesus.

Everyone in the church has their needs met. (Notice that the people cover the needs of others, but not their wants.) Some people even sell property and give the proceeds to the church, to help those in need.

Barnabas, a man from the tribe of Levi, sells a field he owns and gives all the money to the church leaders.

Inspired by his selfless act, and no doubt enamored by the attention it receives, Ananias and his wife, Sapphira, also sell a piece of property. They keep some of the money for themselves—something they have every right to do—but they pretend that the part they give to the church is 100 percent of the sale.

They're posers. They pretend to be generous when they're not. They seek to earn praise for their charity, but they selfishly scheme to keep some of the money for themselves.

Peter's not pleased with their duplicity and neither is God.

With supernatural insight into what they did, Peter confronts Ananias. Peter boldly accuses him of having his heart controlled by Satan and lying to the Holy Spirit. These are serious charges. What they did in secret—withholding some of their money while pretending to give it all—is known by God and Peter. Soon the whole church will know too. "You didn't just lie to the church but to God," Peter says. "How could you have done such a thing?"

When Ananias hears Peter's rebuff, he drops dead.

That gets everyone's attention. Fear overcomes the believers. Some men carry off Ananias's body and bury him.

Three hours later, Sapphira walks in, not knowing the fate of her husband. Peter gives her a chance to come clean. She doesn't. Peter accuses her of conspiring against the Holy Spirit. Just then the men who buried her husband return from their task. She, too, drops dead. The men carry her out and bury her next to her husband.

A holy fear of God's power grips the church.

For Ananias and Sapphira, judgment is instant. They tried to cheat God and didn't get a second chance to make things right.

What can we do to balance our love for God with a healthy fear of his omnipotent sovereignty?

[Discover more about giving in 2 Corinthians 9:6–8.]

DAY 9: MORE HEALING AND MORE PERSECUTION
ACTS 5:12–42

The apostles left the Sanhedrin, rejoicing because they had
been counted worthy of suffering disgrace for the Name.
(Acts 5:41)

In Acts 3:1–4:4 we learn how, when Peter miraculously heals the lame man, the opportunity opens for him to tell others about Jesus. We often see this connection in the book of Acts, that miracle healings provide a path for people to hear what missionaries say about Jesus.

There's also another common connection. Persecution. When God's power is most visibly present, opposition often occurs. As a result, God's people face persecution. When Peter and John heal the lame man, they end up in jail. Though they only spend the night there before their release—without charges—it is a form of persecution.

Though this persecution sometimes comes from nonreligious people, too often the attacks come from their Jewish brothers. This is sad. People who believe in the same God and pursue him with diligence have harassed and even killed those who have a different perspective about him.

When Peter heals the lame man in the name of Jesus, the Church grows. After their release from jail, Peter and John pray for more boldness in what they say and for more supernatural power to heal people and perform miracles.

God answers their prayer, and they perform many more miracles. Their numbers increase as more men and women believe. Guess what else happens?

Yep. More persecution.

The Jewish religious leaders grow jealous of all the attention garnered by Team Jesus. Unable to see the hand of God—the God they worship—at work, they go on the offensive against the apostles. They arrest some of them and toss them in jail.

This time the religious leaders don't release their prisoners. Instead, God does. He sends an angel to the jail who opens the door and lets them out. "Go to the temple," the angel says, "and tell everyone there about Jesus."

The next day, when the religious council sends for the prisoners, the guards find their cell empty. Instead, the apostles are in the temple teaching about Jesus. Out of fear of reprisal from the people, the guards don't use force and instead ask the apostles to come with them to appear before the religious council. Peter and company agree, and they're chewed out again for talking about Jesus—and blaming the religious leaders for his death.

Peter again reminds the Council that he and the other followers of Jesus must obey God instead of religious authority. And Peter once more reminds them that they did indeed execute Jesus. This infuriates them, and they want to kill the apostles, but Gamaliel, a wise teacher of the Law, speaks common sense to them. "Don't do anything to these people," he warns. "If they're acting on their own accord, it will soon fail. But if God is behind it, you'll never stop it, and we'll end up fighting him."

He persuades them to not kill the apostles and let them go. But they get a sound beating first.

The apostles leave, celebrating that they were worthy of facing persecution in Jesus's name.

Are the things we do for Jesus worthy of us facing persecution?

[Discover more about persecution in Romans 8:35, 2 Corinthians 12:10, Hebrews 10:33, and Revelation 2:10.]

DIG DEEPER: THE POWER OF PETER'S SHADOW

As a result, people brought the sick into the streets and laid them on beds and mats so that at least Peter's shadow might fall on some of them as he passed by. (Acts 5:15)

Whan Luke writes about the amazing supernatural wonders the apostles do, he slips in a curious one-liner. He says the people line the road with their sick friends, hoping for Peter's shadow to fall on them as he walks by.

Luke doesn't confirm that Peter's shadow does in fact heal people.

It could be these people act out of superstition, thinking Peter's shadow has healing abilities. Or, more likely, they know that Peter's shadow healed people in the past, and they hope it will happen again. We don't know for sure.

However, we do know that Jesus often healed people through physical contact, and once a woman's chronic bleeding stopped when she touched the hem of his robe. Later we'll see Paul impart healing on others when they receive articles of clothing he touched. They're cured and evil spirits leave them—even though Paul isn't present.

Given all this, it's not a stretch to think that Peter's shadow is enough to heal people. Regardless, the Bible shows people healed in the name of Jesus.

Do we believe we can heal people in Jesus's name today? What do we need to do about that?

[Discover more about healing in Luke 5:13, Luke 8:43–44, Luke 22:51, and Acts 19:11–12.]

DAY 10: THE FIRST DEACONS
ACTS 6:1–7

"It would not be right for us to neglect the ministry of the word of God in order to wait on tables." (Acts 6:2)

One of many recurring themes in the book of Acts is that Jesus's church grows. With growth comes challenges, which we can optimistically call opportunities for improvement.

One of the tangible problems with this growth is in fairly distributing food to the people each day. One group of people complain that their widows aren't getting enough to eat. They accuse another group of ignoring them.

Imagine being in the food line and seeing the people in front of you receive much, yet when it comes your turn, you receive little. Or even worse, the food is gone by the time you get there. I've seen this happen to others, and it's happened to me. In my case, there's plenty to eat at home, so I can easily make up the shortfall later. However, for some people, not receiving enough food or not being served at all means going hungry until the next day.

This is not something the twelve disciples want to happen. Yet they're also wise enough to know that if they try to personally deal with this, other areas of ministry will suffer, namely telling people about Jesus.

To address the problem, without creating a new one, they suggest appointing some people to make sure the food is equally shared.

They recommend their community select seven men to head up this task. (Sorry ladies, but the Bible does say men. This would've been a great opportunity for the disciples to move the female population of their church into leadership, but they missed it.)

For qualifications, they don't suggest that these people have organizational skills, have restaurant experience, or even know how to cook. Instead, the requirements are spiritual. They must be full of God's Spirit and wise. With this team in place, the twelve disciples can return their focus to prayer and telling people about Jesus.

Everyone likes this idea.

Luke doesn't explain the selection process. However, given other things we read about in the book of Acts, they might cast lots or reach a consensus, since the early church did those things and doesn't appear to have ever voted about anything. Today's church might want to consider this example of casting lots instead of voting.

Regardless of the method used, in a grassroots effort, they pick seven guys who meet the criteria. The people present the seven to the apostles, who lay hands on them and pray for them. They are the first deacons.

What happens next?

You probably know. With this new infrastructure in place, more people hear about Jesus and the church has another growth spurt.

How might our expectations of what church leaders should do distract them from what's most important?

[Discover more about selecting ministry leaders in Acts 1:26, Acts 15:2, Acts 15:25–27, 2 Timothy 1:11, and Titus 1:5.]

DAY 11: STEPHEN'S SERMON
ACTS 6:8 TO ACTS 7:50

Then the high priest asked Stephen, "Are these charges true?"
(Acts 7:1)

The requirements for the seven deacons are that they should be full of God's Spirit and of wisdom. Of the seven deacons, Stephen stands out. Luke writes that Stephen is a man of much faith, who operates under Holy Spirit power. These seem like lofty credentials for someone to pass out food, yet Stephen handles more than just food.

Like the other apostles, Stephen performs amazing supernatural signs and wonders. Some of the Jews don't like what Stephen is doing, and they oppose him. They argue with him and try to pick a fight. But the Holy Spirit tells him what to say, and no one can stand against him.

Not able to win their battle with logic, they go to plan B. They convince some scoundrels to perjure themselves and lie about Stephen. These rascals accuse Stephen of blasphemy, of slandering both Moses and God. They stir up the people and the religious leaders. The crowd grabs Stephen and drags him before the Council.

Stephen's opponents produce false witnesses. They claim that Stephen speaks against the temple and the Law of Moses, the Torah. Then they levy more fabricated charges against Stephen.

Everyone in the proceeding glares at Stephen. His face shines like an angel.

The high priest asks Stephen, "Are these charges true?"

The answer is "no," but this isn't what Stephen says. Instead he launches into a sermon.

He reminds them of their past as a people. He starts with God's call to Father Abraham and the rite of circumcision. Then there's Abraham's son Isaac and grandson Jacob, father of twelve boys, who later become the twelve tribes. There's Jacob's son Joseph, sold as a slave and ending up in Egypt.

Then Jacob and sons move to Egypt because they're starving. Their descendants stay there for four hundred years and end up enslaved. Along comes Moses, a baby who is no ordinary child. As an adult, he encounters God in a burning bush. Moses eventually leads God's chosen people out of Egypt, and they return to the land God promised to Abraham.

Later there's David and son Solomon, who builds the temple. Along the way, Stephen quotes the prophets Amos and Isaiah. It's a powerful historical overview of some of the Old Testament's key points.

But it doesn't in any way answer the question the high priest asked Stephen.

When wrongly accused, how do we respond? Do we try to clear ourselves or use it as an opportunity to advance God's kingdom?

[Discover more about the Holy Spirit giving us words to say at our trial in Matthew 10:19–20, Mark 13:11, and Luke 12:11–12.]

DIG DEEPER: THE ELEVEN SERMONS IN ACTS

Preach the word. (2 Timothy 4:2)

Paul instructs his protégé Timothy to be ready to preach the word of God, which is to share a testimony or deliver a sermon. The book of Acts has eleven sermons (teachings, messages, and testimonies).

There are three from Peter, one from Stephen, and seven from Paul. Here's a list:

1. Peter speaks at Pentecost (Acts 2:14–36)

2. Peter after he heals a lame man (Acts 3:12–26)

3. Stephen before he's martyred (Acts 7:1–53)

4. Peter speaks to the Gentiles (Acts 10:34–43)

5. Paul speaks at the synagogue in Antioch (Acts 13:16–41)

6. Paul cleverly connects with the people of Athens (Acts 17:22–31)

7. Paul will obey God regardless (Acts 20:18–35)

8. Paul's words stir up the crowd (Acts 22:3–21)

9. Paul's testimony (Acts 24:10–21)

10. Paul's story (Acts 26:2–29)

11. Paul speaks in Rome (Acts 28:23–28)

What can we learn from these sermons?

[Discover more about preaching the good news of Jesus in Luke 16:16, as well as Isaiah 52:7, which Romans 10:15 quotes.]

DAY 12: THEY FORGET TO LEAVE
ACTS 7:51 TO ACTS 8:4

On that day a great persecution broke out against the church in Jerusalem, and all except the apostles were scattered throughout Judea and Samaria. (Acts 8:1)

Everyone listens, without rancor, to what Stephen says in his sermon. Then he starts meddling.

He calls the people a stiff-necked group. He accuses them of having uncircumcised hearts and ears. Being uncircumcised is a major insult. Then he adds that just as their ancestors did, they resist the Holy Spirit, persecuting every prophet that God sent. This includes Jesus, the righteous Son of God, whom they murdered.

This isn't the best way to wrap up a sermon. If Stephen intended to give an altar call, he never gets that far.

At this point the members of the religious council grow enraged. They gnash their teeth at him in righteous anger.

But Stephen, full of the Holy Spirit, looks up. He peers into heaven and sees God. "Look," Stephen points. "I see into heaven. Jesus stands at God's right hand."

The people in the hearing have had enough. They cover their ears, scream, and rush him. In a riotous frenzy, they drag him outside the city and pelt him with rocks.

A man named Saul stands there, witnessing the whole thing and giving his approval. We'll hear more about him later. A lot more.

As the stones hit Stephen and break his body, he's about to die. He asks Jesus to receive his spirit. He falls to his knees, begging God to forgive those killing him. Then he dies.

Some godly men bury Stephen. The people mourn his death.

Emboldened by what happened, a wave of persecution breaks out against the church of Jesus. Most everyone hightails it out of there. They scatter in all directions.

In Jerusalem, Saul goes on a rampage to destroy Jesus's church. He moves from house to house, arresting believers and throwing them in jail.

It seems a dark time for the church. Yet after Stephen's martyrdom, the church does exactly what Jesus had told them to do. He instructed them to wait in Jerusalem until they received the gift of the Holy Spirit from Papa. Then they were supposed to go out and tell others about Jesus. They forgot that part—until now.

Though Jesus told them to wait in Jerusalem, the waiting wasn't indefinite.

There's a time to wait and a time to go. How do we discern which is which?

[Discover more about what Jesus tells his followers to do in Matthew 28:18–20 and Acts 1:4 and 8.]

DIG DEEPER: JESUS STANDS

"Look," he said, "I see heaven open and the Son of Man standing at the right hand of God." (Acts 7:56)

Between Stephen ending his overview of the Old Testament and the crowd becoming so incensed with his words that they kill him, he looks up into heaven and tells the people what he sees.

He sees God in all his glory, with Jesus at his side. But Jesus isn't sitting next to Father God, as the Bible usually describes.

This time Jesus stands. It's as though he rises, ready to welcome Stephen into heaven. Even before Stephen prays for Jesus to receive his spirit when his body dies, Jesus is waiting. He stands, ready to welcome his faithful servant into eternal glory.

Though the Bible doesn't mention it, I imagine Jesus with outstretched arms and a broad smile. He mouths the words, "Welcome home, good and faithful servant."

When our time comes to join Jesus in heaven, may we receive the same greeting.

Will Jesus stand to welcome us?

[Discover more about Jesus in heaven in Matthew 19:28, Matthew 26:64, and Mark 14:61–62.]

DAY 13: NOT ALL THAT'S SUPERNATURAL IS GOOD

ACTS 8:4–25

You have no part or share in this ministry, because your heart is not right before God. (Acts 8:21)

R emember how Jesus's followers scatter after the Jews kill Stephen? Philip goes to Samaria. In Jesus's name, he does amazing supernatural things. He heals people who can't walk and exorcises evil spirits from others. Because of this, the people pay attention to what he says. The city fills with joy over what God does through Philip.

But not all that's supernatural is good.

We learn this from a man named Simon. We

call him Simon the Sorcerer. He also lives in Samaria. He's an accomplished wizard and impresses everyone with the amazing feats he performs. He boasts in his witchcraft abilities and claims to be someone great. All the people in this town think highly of him and his supernatural power. They've followed him for some time.

When Philip shows up, things change. The people listen to what he says. They believe in Jesus and the kingdom of God. To confirm their belief, they're baptized. Even Simon believes and is baptized. Impressed with Philip's supernatural power, Simon follows him everywhere.

Hearing what's happening in Samaria, Peter and John show up to check things out. They pray for the new believers to receive the Holy Spirit, because they had only been baptized in Jesus's name. When Peter and John place their hands on the Samaritan believers, they receive the Holy Spirit too, just like what happened at Pentecost.

When Simon sees how the touch of Peter and John imparts the Holy Spirit to others, Simon wants this ability too. He offers to buy this power, no doubt eager to add it to the supernatural abilities he's learned as a sorcerer.

He doesn't understand.

He wants to combine spiritual practices that shouldn't be comingled—that can't merge. The Holy Spirit has no part in sorcery. The two don't mix. They're mutually exclusive. The spiritual practices of following Jesus stand alone. Adding other supernatural pursuits don't enhance the journey as a disciple of Jesus. Instead they distract from it.

Even worse, Simon wants to buy Holy Spirit power. But the Holy Spirit is not for sale. Remember, the Holy Spirit is a gift sent to Team Jesus from Papa. Emphasis on gift.

Peter knows this. He harshly condemns Simon. Simon believes in Jesus and was baptized, but his heart isn't right. He's not fit for ministry. "Repent of your wickedness," Peter says. "Beg God to forgive you, because I see that you're not right with him and headed in the wrong direction."

Implicitly Simon does repent when he asks Peter to pray for him. However, Luke doesn't record the outcome of Peter's prayer. This leaves us to speculate on Simon's fate.

Are there unbiblical spiritual practices that we have wrongly added to our faith in Jesus? In what ways have we tried to buy God's favor?

[Discover more about sorcery in Deuteronomy 18:10, Deuteronomy 18:14, Malachi 3:5, Acts 13:6–12, and Acts 19:19.]

DIG DEEPER: EVIL SPIRITS AND MENTAL ILLNESS

Their illnesses were cured and the evil spirits left them. (Acts 19:12)

I n the Bible we run across the phrase "evil spirit," along with "demon-possessed," and "impure spirit."

Evil spirit occurs twelve times in the Bible, six in Luke's writings (the books of Luke and Acts). *Demon-possessed* occurs twenty-one times in the Bible, five in Luke's two books. *Impure spirit* occurs twenty-six times in the Bible, nine from Dr. Luke.

What is an evil spirit? Is it the same as demon possession? Maybe.

Consider these four ideas about understanding evil spirits and demon possession.

- As a teenager, I thought an evil spirit and demon possession were ancient man's way of grasping mental illness.
- As a young adult, my perspective flipped. I thought mental illness was modern man's attempt to explain evil spirits and demon possession, apart from spirituality.
- Later I considered that both mental illness and evil spirits/demon possession existed but as different phenomena.
- Now I wonder if these are just two ways of looking at the same thing—one from a spiritual viewpoint and the other from a secular perspective. This, of course, is speculation. That's why I said that I wonder. I don't know. Thankfully, God does.

Although debating the meaning of evil spirits and demon possession might be an interesting intellectual discussion, the main point is that Jesus makes the lives of people with evil spirits and demon possession better. And he gives his followers the authority to do the same thing.

How should we understand evil spirits and demon possession today?

[Discover more about evil spirits in 1 Samuel 16:14–23, 1 Samuel 18:10, 1 Samuel 19:9, Luke 7:21, Luke 8:2, and Acts 19:11–16. Learn more about demon possession in Luke 8:26–38 and Luke 9:37–42.]

DAY 14: PHILIP AND THE ETHIOPIAN TREASURER

ACTS 8:26–40

Now an angel of the Lord said to Philip, "Go south to the road—the desert road." (Acts 8:26)

Though God's doing amazing work in Samaria through Philip, God doesn't have him stick around to help the people grow in their new faith. Instead, God sends an angel to tell Philip to leave. "Take the desert road and head south," the angel says.

From a human standpoint, this makes no sense. Philip's in the middle of a major revival. He's performing miracles, telling people about Jesus, and seeing Jesus's church grow. Why leave all that and head out into the desert where there are few people, if any?

To his credit, Philip doesn't question the angel's instructions. He obeys, even though he may not understand why God wants him to leave.

As he heads south, he meets an Ethiopian official, the treasurer for the queen. The man is returning home from a religious pilgrimage in Jerusalem. He sits in his chariot reading from Isaiah's prophecy.

The Holy Spirit nudges Philip: "Approach the chariot." Philip runs up and asks the Ethiopian if he understands what he's reading.

The man shakes his head. "Can you explain it?"

Philip joins the Ethiopian in his chariot.

The passage prophesies about Jesus, but the man doesn't realize it. He wonders if Isaiah is writing about himself or someone else.

Starting with that passage, Philip tells the Ethiopian about Jesus, explaining things more thoroughly and answering the man's questions.

As they travel along in the chariot, they come upon some water. "Look at that," the man says. "Is there any reason why you can't baptize me?"

He stops the chariot and the two men walk into the water. Philip baptizes him. That's the end of their interaction, because after baptizing the man, Philip finds himself supernaturally whisked away to his next mission.

As for the Ethiopian treasurer, he's unfazed by Philip's sudden disappearance. He continues his journey home, full of joy. He'll have much to share with his family and friends—as well as with leaders in the Ethiopian government—when he arrives. We can only speculate on the scope of his influence there, but it could be huge.

How willing are we to obey the Holy Spirit's instructions when it makes no sense? Do we move forward with reluctance or in expectation?

[Discover what the Ethiopian treasurer read in Isaiah 53:7–8.]

DAY 15: SAUL MAKES A U-TURN
ACTS 9:1–31

"Brother Saul, the Lord—Jesus, who appeared to you on the road as you were coming here—has sent me so that you may see again and be filled with the Holy Spirit." (Acts 9:17)

T hink back to when the Jews stoned Stephen to death. Remember who witnessed the whole thing and gave his approval? Saul. With holy zeal, Saul then goes on a rampage, doing whatever he can to squelch the good news of Jesus and put an end to his church.

Taking a lead role in persecuting followers of Jesus, he does what he can in Jerusalem. However, the people have scattered throughout the area, so

PETER DEHAAN

Saul takes his vendetta on the road. Armed with written authority from the high priest, Saul heads to Damascus to disrupt Jesus's church in that city too. He plans to search for followers of Jesus and drag them as prisoners back to Jerusalem.

God has other plans.

How encouraging is that? Our plans mean nothing when God has other ideas.

As Saul and his entourage travel to Damascus, a bright light flashes. He falls to the ground. A voice asks, "Saul, why are you harassing me?"

"Who are you, sir?"

"I'm Jesus, the one you're persecuting," the voice says. "Get up, go into the city, and wait for instructions."

Saul's traveling companions don't know what to make of this. They hear the voice, but they don't see a thing. They lead Saul into Damascus because he can't see. This may be due to the bright light or his encounter with Jesus. Blinded, Saul fasts for three days.

As Saul waits, God is at work. In a vision, he appears to his disciple Ananias. He tells Ananias where Saul is staying and to go heal him. Ananias objects. He's heard about Saul and knows of his mission. By getting anywhere near this murderous persecutor, Ananias risks jail, even death. The wise choice is to flee in the opposite direction.

But God repeats his command to go, and Ananias does.

He finds Saul and heals him. Saul's sight returns, and the Holy Spirit fills him. He's baptized and ends his three-day fast.

After spending time with the believers in Damascus, Saul begins telling others about Jesus, instead of opposing him. Astonished, the people are confused. The Jews conspire to kill Saul, but he escapes and returns to Jerusalem, a changed man. However, the church in Jerusalem is understandably wary of his conversion.

Along comes Barnabas. He boldly sides with Saul, placing the entire Jerusalem church at risk. Eventually they realize Saul's a changed man, that his life mission made a U-turn. They accept him.

The church of Jesus continues to grow stronger and enjoys a time of peace. But this wouldn't have happened had it not been for the bold, faith-filled actions of Ananias and Barnabas.

Are we willing to take great personal risk to obey God? Do we push common sense aside to do what God says?

[Discover more about Barnabas in Galatians 2:1–13 and Colossians 4:10.]

DAY 16: HEALING AND RESURRECTION

ACTS 9:32–43

Turning toward the dead woman, he said, "Tabitha, get up."
She opened her eyes, and seeing Peter she sat up. (Acts 9:40)

N ow we return to the story of Peter. We're about to see two more examples of the power of God at work among his people.

Traveling the country, Peter stops at Lydda to check in on the believers there. He meets Aeneas, who hasn't been able to walk for eight years. We don't know what happened to him, whether an accident or disease, but the paralyzed man is bedridden.

Peter says to him, "Be healed in Jesus's name. Get up!"

Aeneas does.

The people in Lydda spot Aeneas walking around, and they turn to follow Jesus.

It's heartening to see how Peter changed Aeneas's life, by restoring his ability to walk. He does this in the name of Jesus.

What's confounding, however, is that the other believers living in Lydda haven't done this or can't do this. Aeneas has been lying in bed for eight years, waiting for the healing power of Jesus to enable him to walk again. No one helps him until Peter comes along.

In nearby Joppa lives a disciple, named Tabitha, which is Dorcas in Greek. She spends her time helping others. But she gets sick. She dies. Her friends hold a wake for her.

Hearing that Peter is in Lydda, the disciples in Joppa send for him. They ask him to come right away. He does.

When he arrives, Tabitha's body lies there for viewing. The people mourn her passing. In appreciation for her life, they show each other the clothes she made for them.

Peter sends them out of the room. He says to

the corpse, "Get up." Tabitha's dead body opens its eyes and she sits up. Peter helps her to her feet and presents her to the believers who are mourning her death. Now they can celebrate her new life.

As this news spreads, more people believe in Jesus. Peter sticks around for a while, staying with Simon, the tanner.

Again we see a person needing the power of Jesus, but the believers in town don't, or can't, act on their own. All they can do is send for Peter. Peter restores Tabitha's life, giving her more time to help others and to do good.

Jesus gave his followers the power and authority to heal others. Some of them embrace this and others do not.

Do we have Jesus's power and authority in us to heal others in his name today? What about raising the dead?

[Discover more about healing faith in Matthew 17:14–20, Mark 9:14–29, and Luke 10:19–20.]

DAY 17: TWO VISIONS FORETELL A NEW THING

ACTS 10

"God has shown me that I should not call anyone impure or unclean." (Acts 10:28)

Cornelius, who is both a Roman centurion (which makes him a Gentile) and a God-fearing man, helps people in need and prays each day. One afternoon he has a vision. In his vision, one of God's angels affirms his generosity and his prayers. "Send for Simon Peter in Joppa. He's staying with Simon the tanner." Cornelius selects three trusted men and sends them to fetch Peter.

The next day, as Peter waits for his meal, he

prays. He has a vision too. In his vision, a large sheet, held by its four corners, drops from heaven. Cradled inside are all kinds of animals—animals the law of Moses prohibits Jews from eating. A voice says, "Peter, get up, kill, and feed your hunger."

"No way!" Peter says. "I never have and never will eat anything the Scriptures says not to, anything that's unclean."

The vision repeats two more times.

As Peter ponders what this means, the men sent by Cornelius show up. The Holy Spirit alerts Peter, "Three men are looking for you. I sent them and want you to go with them."

The next day, Peter and the three men head out. In expectation of Peter's arrival, Cornelius has gathered his relatives and friends.

As a good Jew, it's unlikely Peter's ever been inside the home of a Gentile. But he goes inside Cornelius's house anyway, even though it's contrary to the religious law. He does this with confidence because his vision made it clear to not call anyone unclean.

Until now, Jesus's followers had only shared his good news with other Jews (and some Samaritans) but not Gentiles. To do so would stand as an anathema to their religious heritage.

Peter speaks to the crowd, all Gentiles. He shares with them the readjustment God has just made to his theology. "I now realize God doesn't play favorites. He accepts anyone and everyone who will follow him." Peter tells them about Jesus, about his execution, death, and victory over death. "Everyone who believes in him will have their sins forgiven."

As Peter speaks, the Holy Spirit comes upon everyone in the room. They talk in tongues and praise God. Peter's entourage is shocked that Gentiles can have Holy Spirit power too. Since they've already received Holy Spirit baptism, they then undergo the ceremony of water baptism.

God is doing a new thing. When Jesus said to go into all the world and tell everyone, that's exactly what he meant. Jesus isn't just for the Jews but for the Gentiles too. Everyone. The entire world.

This is good news for me because I'm a Gentile. Maybe you are too.

Who is God telling us to reach out to? Someone we would have otherwise ignored?

[Discover more about sharing the news of Jesus in Matthew 28:19–20, Mark 16:15–16, Luke 14:23, and Acts 1:7–8.]

DAY 18: DEALING WITH DISAGREEMENT

ACTS 11:1–18

"Who was I to think that I could stand in God's way?"
(Acts 11:17)

God has just shown Peter that Jesus is for everyone, both Jew *and* Gentile. First, God revealed this to him supernaturally through a vision. Then God revealed it to him tangibly by giving the Holy Spirit to Gentiles.

Peter knows this and accepts it. But not everyone is so open-minded and ready for God to do a new thing.

This news, that the Gentiles can be saved and receive the Holy Spirit, spreads quickly through the church of Jesus. It's huge. It may be the biggest thing to happen since Jesus rose victorious over his death. Certainly it's the biggest thing to happen to the church since Pentecost.

Yet, as often happens when God does a new thing, criticism arises from people who like the old way. This time the disapproval comes from circumcised believers. "How dare you enter the house of an uncircumcised man. To make things worse, you even ate with them."

Yes, everything Peter did at Cornelius's was contrary to the religious law and Jewish tradition. He associated with Gentiles (who are uncircumcised), entered their home (thereby making himself unclean), and shared a meal with them (something unthinkable). This was all Peter's detractors could see. They missed the bigger news that Gentiles are part of God's plan too. As the saying goes, "They couldn't see the forest for the trees."

Circumcision was a big deal for the Jews, at least for the men. It was more than a religious ceremony that all Jewish boys underwent. It was a rite that spiritually connected them with God and tangibly separated them from all other people, collectively known as Gentiles. It served as a mark of distinction and a source of pride.

However, despite their closed-mindedness, they give Peter a chance to speak.

Peter unveils the whole story to them starting at the beginning: In Joppa praying, a vision, and a strange command to eat unclean food. Three times for emphasis. Three Gentiles, unclean men, show up. God says to go with them, and Peter does. He enters Cornelius's Gentile home and speaks to his Gentile family and friends. He tells them about Jesus, and the Holy Spirit shows up and comes upon the Gentiles. Then Peter has them baptized. "If Papa gave them the same gift that he gave us, who am I to object?"

Peter's explanation addresses their concerns, and they praise God. "Who would have thought it? Even Gentiles can be saved."

When God does a new thing, are we the first to embrace it, or are we quick to oppose it?

[Discover more about circumcision in Genesis 17:10–14, Romans 3:28–30, Romans 4:9–11, and Colossians 3:11.]

DAY 19: JESUS CAME FOR EVERYONE

ACTS 11:19–30

The disciples were called Christians first at Antioch. (Acts 11:26)

After Stephen's martyrdom, Jesus's followers travel to tell others about him —just as he told them to do. But, aside from Peter, they've only shared his good news with other Jews.

That's about to change. Some of them go to Antioch and tell the Gentiles there about Jesus. God blesses their initiative and many people believe.

How amazing is that? First there's Peter telling the Gentile Cornelius and his family about Jesus. Now there are Gentile believers in Antioch too.

The news of what's happening in Antioch spreads fast. It soon makes its way to the church in Jerusalem. They dispatch Barnabas to check things out. When he arrives in Antioch, he sees all that God is doing. This fills Barnabas with joy, and he encourages them to persevere in their faith. His name, by the way, means *son of encouragement*. It seems this is a well-deserved description of his character.

As a result of Barnabas's work in Antioch, a great many more people believe in Jesus. Jesus's church continues to grow, because of the dedicated work of his faithful followers.

Then Barnabas has an idea.

He goes to Tarsus to look for Saul. He finds his friend and brings him back to Antioch. It could be that Barnabas wanted help to do all that needed doing in Antioch, and he knew Saul would be perfect for the job. Or it might be that he saw this as an opportunity to mentor Saul, teaching him through example. Of course, it could be a combination of these two. Saul could contribute to the work of God in Antioch, as well as learn from Barnabas how to be a more effective minister.

Though this is the first time the two of them

work together, it won't be the last. And this is a good thing for the church of Jesus.

In writing about the church in Antioch, Luke slips in an interesting side note. In Antioch the disciples are first called Christians. Interestingly, the word Christian only appears a couple other times in the Bible.

Until now, the followers of Jesus were Jewish and identified with the Jewish faith, perhaps as a new sect of Judaism, like the Pharisees and Sadducees. However, in Antioch, when Greeks begin following Jesus, this doesn't fit into Judaism. The word Christian emerges. It means belonging to the party of Christ. That is, Jesus's party.

Do you like or dislike the label Christian? If you identify with Jesus, what name do you use to describe your faith?

[Discover more about being a Christian in 1 Peter 4:16.]

DAY 20: THE POWER OF PRAYER
WITH AN ELEMENT OF DOUBT

ACTS 12:1–17

*"You're out of your mind," they told her. When she kept
insisting that it was so, they said, "It must be his angel."*
(Acts 12:15)

After Saul decides to stop fighting Jesus and follow him, the church enjoys a time of peace, one with little persecution. Then King Herod gets involved. To harass Jesus's church, Herod arrests John's brother James and executes him. This pleases the Jewish leaders, so Herod grabs Peter next, hoping to earn more favor by killing him too.

This happens during the Passover, which is an

inconvenient time for a trial and execution, so Herod puts Peter in prison, guarded by sixteen soldiers. Once the Passover celebration is over, Herod will try Peter with the expectation of another execution.

This is the third time Peter's been in jail for serving Jesus. Peter's first arrest happened after he healed a lame man. They released Peter because they couldn't deny what happened, and all the people were praising God.

The second time, a group of apostles, including Peter, was imprisoned. An angel rescues them, unlocking the doors and letting them out. It's a supernatural jailbreak.

Will God intervene again to free Peter or will Herod prevail in killing his prisoner, just as he did with James?

The church gathers to pray for Peter. They intercede in earnest. For most of us, our prayers today seldom address life or death issues, but for Peter, that's exactly what he faces. Without divine intervention he will surely die.

As Peter languishes in prison, the church prays. The night before his trial begins, an angel appears. The cell lights up. The angel nudges Peter to rouse him. Chained between two soldiers, the restraints fall off without waking the guards.

"Quick," the angel says. "Get dressed and follow me."

Peter thinks it's a vision. They pass two sets of guards and reach an iron gate. It opens by itself, and they move through. They walk down the street. Then the angel disappears.

Peter realizes it's not a vision and that he's free. He heads to Mary's house, which is where Team Jesus is having their prayer meeting. He knocks, anxious to get off the street before soldiers find and recapture him.

Rhoda, one of the believers who is praying for Peter, goes to the door. She hears his voice and, full of excitement, runs back to tell everyone that Peter is safe. But in her haste, she neglects to unlatch the door.

The people earnestly praying for Peter don't believe her. Even though they pray in faith, they have a sliver of doubt that doesn't allow them to accept that God answered their prayers.

Peter keeps knocking, and they finally let him in. They're shocked. He updates them on what happened and leaves town in a hurry.

How do we understand faith and doubt?

[Discover more about God's divine intervention for his imprisoned servants in Acts 5:18–19 and Acts 16:22–28.]

DIG DEEPER: THE TWELVE DISCIPLES IN ACTS

When morning came, he called his disciples to him and chose twelve of them. (Luke 6:13)

Remember that Jesus started with twelve disciples. Then one of them, Judas Iscariot, betrayed him and committed suicide out of remorse, bringing the number down to eleven. That left:

1. Peter
2. John
3. James
4. Andrew
5. Philip
6. Thomas

7. Bartholomew

8. Matthew

9. James, son of Alphaeus

10. Simon the Zealot

11. Judas, son of James

Then the disciples add Matthias to fill Judas's slot. This restores the number of disciples to twelve, which is symbolically significant, connecting the twelve disciples with the twelve tribes of Israel.

However, Herod arrests and kills James, bringing the number back to eleven. The Bible doesn't mention if they find a replacement for James.

Why do you think the disciples replaced Judas but not James?

[Discover more about the changing number of disciples in Matthew 27:3–5, Acts 1:23–26, and Acts 12:2.]

DAY 21: THE PRIDE OF HEROD
ACTS 12:18–24

Immediately, because Herod did not give praise to God, an angel of the Lord struck him down, and he was eaten by worms and died. (Acts 12:23)

After God answers the church's prayer and Peter receives a divine jailbreak, the next morning there's quite a commotion in the prison. Where's Peter? The guards have no idea. Herod investigates thoroughly and executes the guards.

Then he leaves town. He goes to Caesarea. This might be a getaway of sorts. He stays there a while. He may hope to forget what happened in Jerusalem after his plans to kill Peter failed.

Herod's been having an ongoing quarrel with the people from Tyre and Sidon. They seek an audience with him. They want to put their differences behind them because he controls the food supply, which they need to survive.

They set a day to meet and resolve their differences. Herod shows up dressed in his royal robes. He sits on the throne, showing his power, an imposing presence. He addresses them. We don't know what he says or if it's even an impressive oration. But we do know how the people who want to garner his favor respond.

In a raucous reaction, they applaud. "This is no mere man. It's like we just heard the voice of a god!"

Full of arrogance, Herod accepts their excessive praise and their unwarranted approval of his speech. After his failure to bring about Peter's death, Herod may think he's due for a win. He's willing to receive their adoration and bask in the glory they're giving him. Though he should correct their tribute and redirect their praise to God, he doesn't.

God isn't pleased.

An angel strikes Herod. Worms eat at his body, and he dies. This is surely a painful, agonizing end.

The outcome of death that Herod intended for Peter, he receives himself.

Although God doesn't strike down all his enemies like he did with Herod, he can do it. In Herod's case, God has had enough. He isn't willing to let any more of his people die at the hands of this tyrant.

When have we received praise for ourselves that we should have given to God?

[Discover more about the affliction of worms in Job 7:5, Isaiah 14:11, and Mark 9:47–48, which quotes Isaiah 66:24.]

DAY 22: A HOLY SPIRIT ASSIGNMENT
ACTS 12:25 TO ACTS 13:52

While they were worshiping the Lord and fasting, the Holy Spirit said, "Set apart for me Barnabas and Saul for the work to which I have called them." (Acts 13:2)

Our narrative of the early church now returns to Barnabas and Saul, also called Paul. In Antioch, as the church worships God and fasts, the Holy Spirit gives them instructions. "I have an assignment for Barnabas and Saul. Bless them, and send them out."

When the church completes their fast, they place their hands on the two, dispatching them for their new adventure. It's their first missionary journey.

The Holy Spirit sends the pair, joined by John Mark, to Seleucia, then Cyprus, and on to Salamis. They go to the synagogues and tell the Jews about Jesus.

On Paphos they meet a Jewish sorcerer, a false prophet, named Bar-Jesus (Elymas). Elymas opposes them and tries to turn his boss, the proconsul, from his faith in Jesus. Saul, who now goes by Paul, has a spiritual smackdown with Elymas. Guided by Holy Spirit insight, Paul calls Elymas a child of the devil, an enemy to all that is right. "You're full of deceit and tricks. Stop perverting God's ways." Paul says God will blind Elymas for a time. Immediately Elymas loses his sight. That gets his attention and amazes his boss.

Next Barnabas and Paul go to Perga and then Pisidian Antioch (a different city than Antioch in Syria). On the Sabbath, they go to the synagogue. The leaders ask if they have anything to share. Paul does. He preaches a sermon, connecting their history and their scriptures to explain about Jesus. Paul quotes several passages and wraps up by citing Habakkuk, who prophesies that God will do a new thing.

As the meeting wraps up, the people invite Paul and Barnabas to come back the next week. They do. Most of the city shows up to hear what they have to say. Some of the Jews, however, grow jealous and oppose Paul, arguing against what he says.

Paul and Barnabas have an answer, a somber one. "We wanted to tell you Jews about Jesus, first. But because you won't listen and reject this good news, we'll tell the Gentiles instead." The Gentiles are overjoyed and begin following Jesus.

This is the third time where it's made clear that Jesus didn't come just for the Jews, but for everyone. This is good news indeed.

Jesus came for everyone, but do our actions truly show that we believe this?

[Discover more about God's desire for everyone to come to him in Isaiah 2:2, Isaiah 42:6, Isaiah 49:6, Obadiah 1:15, Haggai 2:7, and Matthew 28:19.]

DIG DEEPER: SAUL, ALSO
CALLED PAUL

Then Saul, who was also called Paul, filled with the Holy Spirit, looked straight at Elymas. (Acts 13:9)

In the book of Acts, Luke uses two names for the same person, but he never bothers to tell us why. We mostly know this person as Paul, but Luke first calls him Saul.

We meet Saul in Acts 7. His name occurs twenty-nine times in the New Testament, all in the first part of Acts.

(Note that in the Old Testament, Israel's first king is also Saul. Yup, there are two guys named Saul in the Bible. Interestingly, Paul/Saul mentions

King Saul in his message to the people of Pisidian Antioch.)

In Acts 13, Luke writes "Saul, also called Paul." Luke doesn't explain the reason for this name switch. Was Saul always known as Paul? Did Saul decide to change his name to Paul? Is there a spiritual or practical reason for this switch? We're left to wonder.

After writing that Saul is also called Paul, Luke uses Paul for the rest of the book of Acts. The name Paul occurs 183 times in Acts and a total of 239 times in the New Testament.

Do people know us by different names? Is there a spiritual or practical reason for this?

[Discover more about King Saul in 1 Samuel 9, 1 Samuel 15:10–11, and Acts 13:21, as well as over 300 other verses in the Old Testament.]

DAY 23: PAUL TAKES A LEAD ROLE
ACTS 14

Paul looked directly at him, saw that he had faith to be healed and called out, "Stand up on your feet!" At that, the man jumped up and began to walk. (Acts 14:9–10)

After Paul and Barnabas preach to the Gentiles about Jesus in Pisidian Antioch, producing impressive results, they do the same thing in Iconium. There, both Jews and Gentiles believe in Jesus. After spending much time there to build the growing church, a plot emerges to silence them. They leave town and head for Lystra.

In Lystra, Paul heals a man who had been lame from birth. The locals think Paul and Barnabas are gods. It's all the pair can do to keep the people from offering sacrifices to them. Some of the Jews who harassed them in Pisidian Antioch and Iconium arrive to stir up more trouble. A mob forms, and they stone Paul, dragging him outside the city, presumed dead. But with the disciples gathered around his body, Paul gets up and walks back to the city. The next day he and Barnabas head for Derbe, where many more people decide to follow Jesus.

Then they backtrack to revisit the disciples they left in Lystra, Iconium, and Pisidian Antioch.

At each city church, they appoint elders. There are no nominations or voting, but prayer and fasting is part of the selection process. Then they dedicate the elders' work for God.

After a time in Pisidian Antioch, Paul and Barnabas head out again. They go to Pisidia, Pamphylia, Perga, and Attalia, as they return to their home base in Antioch (Syria).

Not only did we see Saul's name change to Paul in the last passage, we also saw the beginning of a change in leadership in this missionary duo. Until then Barnabas had taken the lead role with Paul in a supporting function. Now we see the leadership shift to Paul.

Barnabas's mentorship of Paul has been a success, with Paul now being the primary missionary on their team. Barnabas accepts this change. We see no hint of jealousy, hurt, or conflict on the part of Barnabas, a perspective worthy of emulation.

The two work together for the rest of the trip. They form a powerful missionary team that tells people about Jesus, with remarkable success. From a spiritual perspective, it doesn't matter who's in charge or who does what. It's the kingdom results that matter. It's people turning to Jesus and believing in him that's important. The role each person plays is inconsequential.

Are we willing to put our pride aside for the cause of Jesus?

[Discover more by considering John the Baptist's attitude of his ministry role in respect to Jesus in John 3:30.]

DIG DEEPER: PAUL'S FOUR JOURNEYS

You will be my witnesses in Jerusalem, and in all Judea and Samaria, and to the ends of the earth. (Acts 1:8)

Paul, formerly called Saul, does a lot of traveling to tell others about Jesus and encourage believers. In addition to several journeys to Jerusalem, he goes on four long trips. The first three are missionary trips, while the fourth one is as a prisoner.

Paul's first missionary journey, with Barnabas (Acts 13:1 to Acts 15:35):

- Antioch
- Selucia

- Cyprus
- Salamis
- Paphos
- Perga (in Pamphylia)
- Pisidia Antioch
- Iconium
- Lystra
- Derbe
- Lystra
- Iconium
- Pisidia Antioch
- Perga
- Attalia
- Returns to Antioch

Paul's second missionary journey, with Silas (Acts 15:36 to Acts 18:22):

- Antioch
- Cilicia
- Derbe
- Lystra
- Phrygia
- Galatia
- Troas

- Samothrace
- Neapolis
- Philippi (stays several days)
- Amphipolis
- Apollonia
- Thessalonica
- Berea
- Athens
- Corinth (stays a year and a half)
- Cenchreae
- Ephesus (stays two years)
- Caesarea
- Jerusalem
- Returns to Antioch

Paul's third missionary journey, with Luke and possibly others—as shown by the first-person use of *we* (Acts 18:23 to Acts 21:17):

- Antioch
- Galatia and Phrygia
- Ephesus (stays three months)
- Macedonia
- Greece (stays three months)
- Macedonia

- Philippi
- Troas (stays seven days)
- Assos
- Mitylene
- Chios
- Samos
- Miletus
- Kos
- Rhodes
- Patara
- Tyre (stays seven days)
- Ptolemais
- Caesarea
- Jerusalem

Paul's journey to Rome, again, with Luke and perhaps others (Acts 27:1 to Acts 28:16):

- Caesarea (in jail for two years)
- Sidon
- Myra
- Fair Havens (near Lasea)
- Malta (shipwrecked; stays three months)
- Syracuse
- Rhegium

- Puteoli
- Rome (under guard for two years, which is the last we hear about Paul in the Bible)

How many places are we willing to visit to tell others about Jesus?

[Discover more about Paul's plans to travel for Jesus in Romans 15:24.]

DAY 24: DEALING WITH THEOLOGICAL DISAGREEMENTS

ACTS 15:1–35

Then some of the believers who belonged to the party of the Pharisees stood up and said, "The Gentiles must be circumcised and required to keep the law of Moses." (Acts 15:5)

Until now, the church has enjoyed much unity. They've gotten along, just as Jesus prayed they would. And they quickly resolved the one small, potentially divisive issue that arose about food distribution. Now they face a more challenging issue: theological disagreement. Will they overcome it, or will it cause division?

Some people from Judea show up at Antioch. Luke doesn't tell us who these people are, and it's just as well that we don't know. They insist that the path to Jesus must be through Judaism. They specifically require the circumcision of converts, as commanded in the Law of Moses.

This isn't the first time the circumcision issue has come up. In Acts 11:1–18 (see "18: Dealing with Disagreement"), this issue arose, and the church dealt with it quickly. The result was a consensus that Gentiles can be part of the church and don't have to undergo the Jewish rite of circumcision.

However, it seems that not everyone is aware of this decision, or at least they don't care about it. Some of the Pharisees who follow Jesus insist that Gentiles who want to join them must undergo circumcision and keep the Law of Moses.

The church leaders in Jerusalem get together to consider this issue—again.

Peter reminds them of his experience at Cornelius's house, when the Holy Spirit came upon the Gentiles there. As non-Jews, they weren't circumcised, and no one required them to undergo this ritual. Nor did they have to follow Jewish law. The simple requirement was that they believe in Jesus and follow him.

Then Barnabas and Paul share their experience

working with Gentiles and all the supernatural things God did to bring these people into his church.

Next James, likely the brother of Jesus, speaks. He quotes the prophecy of Amos who predicted that even Gentiles would turn to God. James then summarizes his perspective that the church shouldn't add any unnecessary roadblocks for the Gentiles who want to follow Jesus.

The elders, along with the whole church, agree with James's recommendation. They draft a letter outlining their conclusion. Paul and Barnabas, accompanied by Judas (also called Barsabbas) and Silas, deliver the letter to the church in Antioch. This good news encourages the people. Judas and Silas stick around a while to help the church grow in their faith. Then they return to Jerusalem, leaving Paul and Barnabas to continue the work in Antioch.

When theological disagreements arise, do we allow them to divide us or do we seek consensus to stay united?

[Discover more about Amos's prophecy in Amos 9:11–12.]

DAY 25: PAUL AND BARNABAS BREAK UP

ACTS 15:36–41

They had such a sharp disagreement that they parted company. (Acts 15:39)

The church has successfully dealt with a theological disagreement without causing division. But there's another dispute. This one isn't theological, but personal. The outcome is different.

After working a while with the church in Antioch, Paul suggests to Barnabas that they make a return trip to revisit the towns where they told people about Jesus and established city churches. Barnabas likes the idea and wants to take John Mark, his cousin, with them.

Paul isn't so keen on this. "Don't you remember? He bailed on us last time. It's a mistake to take him again."

They continue to discuss the idea, but instead of reaching a consensus, a sharp divide comes between them. Barnabas wants to offer John Mark grace (undeserved favor) and give him a second chance. Paul doesn't. Unable to resolve their differences, this once successful missionary duo breaks up. They go their separate ways.

It's sad that they can't come to an agreement on this. Surely God's kingdom will not grow as powerfully as it once did when these two worked together.

Though this might be one assumption, what happens tells a different story. Both men choose a new apprentice and head in different directions.

Barnabas takes John Mark, and they go to Cyprus.

Paul picks Silas, and they revisit the churches in Syria and Cilicia.

Paul and Barnabas's decision to end their partnership doesn't reduce their effectiveness in reaching people for Jesus. Instead, it multiplies their impact, for they are now able to cover more territory and tell more folks about Jesus. As a bonus, they mentor more people to move into ministry.

God can use what may seem bad from a human perspective to accomplish good and advance his purposes. We're left to ponder whether God orchestrated this whole thing to accomplish his ends, or if the enemy, Satan, caused Paul and Barnabas to break up, only to have God turn things around to produce a positive outcome.

When have we viewed things negatively from a human perspective and missed the hand of God at work?

[Discover more about John Mark in Acts 12:12, Acts 12:25, Acts 13:13, Colossians 4:10, 2 Timothy 4:11, Philemon 1:23–24, and 1 Peter 5:13. Though not all verses specify John Mark, the context makes it reasonable to assume it's the same person.]

DIG DEEPER: MORE ON CIRCUMCISION

You are to undergo circumcision, and it will be the sign of the covenant between me and you. (Genesis 17:11)

C ircumcision is a recurring theme in the book of Acts, as well as the whole Bible.

In Acts 16, Paul wants to take Timothy on the missionary journey with him and Silas. Timothy has an interesting heritage. His mother is Jewish, while his father is Greek. Because of his mixed parentage, he's not circumcised. This shouldn't be an issue because the church leaders already weighed in on the matter—twice. They decided circumcision is a nonissue.

Yet Paul circumcises Timothy.

We're left to wonder why. But one reasonable explanation is that Timothy's standing as an uncircumcised son of a Greek man may have gotten in the way of him being an effective missionary. Circumcising him removes any distraction that might result from his Greek heritage.

However, later a comparable situation arises with Titus. The response is different. In this case, Paul doesn't circumcise Titus. In this instance, Paul takes a stand to make a point that circumcision isn't a salvation issue.

Since Paul had Timothy circumcised but not Titus, the Bible gives us contradicting views on circumcision. Yet the circumstances are different. Timothy's circumcision facilitated ministry. Titus's non-circumcision made a theological statement.

How do we resolve Bible verses that seem to contradict?

[Discover more about circumcision in Galatians 2:3–5, Galatians 5:2–3, and Galatians 6:15.]

DAY 26: JAILED FOR JESUS

ACTS 16

After they had been severely flogged, they were thrown into prison, and the jailer was commanded to guard them carefully.
(Acts 16:23)

As Paul heads out with his new apprentice, Silas, they go to Derby and then on to Lystra. In Lystra they meet Timothy. Timothy believes in Jesus and is a disciple. The people in the area respect Timothy and say good things about him. Both Silas and Timothy are recurring characters in the early church and in the rest of the New Testament.

Paul invites Timothy to join him and Silas on

their missionary journey. Now Paul has two people to mentor.

Guided by the Holy Spirit, they head out and travel from town to town, ending up in Philippi. On the Sabbath, they don't go to the synagogue. Instead they head to the river where they expect to find a place of prayer. As they tell the women who gather there about Jesus, Lydia, who worships God, responds to their message and is baptized. Then she invites them to stay at her house.

Later, Paul and company return to the place of prayer at the river. There's a slave girl there who tells fortunes. Her owners make a lot of money through her. She follows the missionary team, shouting, "These men are God's servants, showing us how to get saved."

This continues for days and wearies Paul so much that he eventually casts the fortune-telling spirit out of her. The spirit leaves. She can no longer tell people their futures, and her masters can no longer make money by exploiting her ability.

The slave girl's owners drag Paul and Silas before the authorities, accusing them of wrongdoing. The pair are stripped, beaten, and thrown in jail.

Sitting in prison, they pray and sing hymns. A captive audience listens. At midnight there's an earthquake. The prison shakes. The doors fly open. Everyone's chains fall off.

The jailer wakes and, assuming his prisoners have fled, he prepares to kill himself, a fate less severe than what will happen to him for failing his duty. But no one escaped, and Paul yells at him to stop. Trembling, the jailer comes up to Paul. "How can I get saved?"

Paul tells him about Jesus and encourages him and his whole household to believe. They do. They're baptized. Joy abounds.

It's great that the jailer and his family follow Jesus and are baptized. But this wouldn't have happened had Paul and Silas not been in jail. And they wouldn't have been in jail had Paul not cast out the fortune-telling spirit in the slave girl. In a roundabout way, performing a supernatural act ended up with Paul being able to tell others about Jesus.

How much are we willing to go through to tell someone the good news about Jesus?

[Discover more about what Paul endured to tell others about Jesus in 2 Corinthians 11:23–27.]

DIG DEEPER: THE PRESENCE OF LUKE

We got ready at once to leave for Macedonia. (Acts 16:10)

Doctor Luke wrote his biography of Jesus, called Luke, in the third person. This is because he researched the events of Jesus's life and documented them for Theophilus—and for us—to read. He continues this approach in researching the early church that we're reading about in Acts.

However, in Acts 16 we see Luke slip into a first-person narrative in his account. This suggests he is now more than a journalist. He's become a participant, part of the missionary team and a co-laborer for the kingdom of God. We now see Luke taking an active role in the work to grow the church of Jesus. This confirms he witnessed and took part in this and other phases of Paul's work.

There are five more sections in the rest of the book of Acts where Luke writes in the first person. This suggests he is an eyewitness of these events and a participant.

When we tell others about Jesus, is it from a safe distance with a third-person perspective, or are we a first-person eyewitness?

[Discover more about Luke's first-person accounts in Acts 16:10–17, Acts 20:4–15, Acts 21:1–18, Acts 27:1–29, Acts 27:37, and Acts 28:1–16.]

DAY 27: SUFFERING FOR JESUS

ACTS 17

But when the Jews in Thessalonica learned that Paul was preaching the word of God at Berea, some of them went there too, agitating the crowds and stirring them up. (Acts 17:13)

P aul and his team make their way to Thessalonica. For three Sabbaths they go to the synagogue. Using the Scriptures, they explain about Jesus and how he had to die and rise again. Some Jews decide to follow Jesus, as well as many God-fearing Greeks.

Some other Jews, however, are jealous of Paul's influence and seek to make trouble for him. They round up some scoundrels, form a mob, and start a riot. Looking for Paul and Silas, they search Jason's house. Paul and Silas aren't there.

Instead the mob grabs Jason and some of the other believers, dragging them before the city leaders and accusing them of being insurgents. Confusion abounds. The city leaders make Jason and the others post bond. Then they let them go. That night Paul and Silas sneak out of town.

They head to Berea. Again, they go to the Jewish synagogue. Luke writes that the people of Berea have a nobler character. When they hear the message of Jesus, they open the Scriptures to make sure that what Paul and Silas say is true. It is. Many Jews believe, along with many Greeks.

But word gets back to the Jews in Thessalonica. They go to Berea to agitate the crowds and stir up more trouble for Paul and his team. The focus of the Jew's angst, Paul leaves town right away. Once Paul is safe, he sends word for Silas and Timothy to join him as soon as possible.

The three reunite in Athens. The city's full of idol worship, which troubles Paul. In the synagogue and in the marketplace, he tells everyone about Jesus and tries to persuade them to follow Jesus. Paul even references one of their altars, dedicated to "an unknown god." He uses it as a springboard to tell them about God, creation, and judgment, with justice coming through Jesus, proved by him rising from the dead.

Though some of the people sneer at the idea of rising from the dead, others believe in Jesus.

In Thessalonica, Berea, and Athens, Paul and his crew endure hostility as they tell others about Jesus, but more people believe anyway. Sometimes suffering accompanies results.

How much are we willing to endure to see the kingdom of God grow?

[Discover more about what Paul is willing to do to win people to Jesus in 1 Corinthians 9:19–23.]

DIG DEEPER: THE WRITINGS
OF PAUL

*This is why I write these things when I am absent, that when
I come I may not have to be harsh in my use of authority.*
(2 Corinthians 13:10)

octor Luke wrote two books in the New
Testament: Luke and Acts. They are the
longest two books and make up about
one quarter of the New Testament's content.

Paul, however, is the most prolific writer in the
New Testament. He wrote thirteen of the New
Testament's twenty-seven books, which is almost
half. His books account for about one third of the
New Testament's content.

Paul's books are all letters. Most are to churches,

while some are to individuals. Here are the letters (books) that Paul wrote:

- Romans
- 1 Corinthians
- 2 Corinthians
- Galatians
- Ephesians
- Philippians
- Colossians
- 1 Thessalonians
- 2 Thessalonians
- 1 Timothy
- 2 Timothy
- Titus
- Philemon

Which of Paul's letters do you like best? Which one challenges you the most?

[Discover more by reading what Peter had to say about Paul's writing in 2 Peter 3:15–16.]

DAY 28: A PROMISE OF PROTECTION
ACTS 18

"Do not be afraid; keep on speaking, do not be silent. For I am with you, and no one is going to attack and harm you."
(Acts 18:9–10)

P aul and company head to Athens and then go to Corinth. There they meet a Jewish couple, Aquila and Priscilla. They're tentmakers, just like Paul. Because they have so much in common, Paul stays with them. Then he devotes himself fulltime to telling the Jews in the area that Jesus is their Savior, but the people won't believe. They oppose Paul and become abusive.

"Your fate is on you," Paul says. "I tried, but

you wouldn't listen. Now I'm going to share this good news of Jesus with the Gentiles."

Despite the opposition from the Jews, many people believe and are baptized. The church of Jesus continues to grow.

One night, God comes to Paul in a vision: "Don't be afraid. Press on. I'll protect you." Based on this promise, Paul stays in Corinth for eighteen months. He teaches them about God. Though Paul's opponents continue to harass him and even drag him before Gallio, the proconsul, God's pledge to keep Paul safe remains. Through it all, God protects Paul and no harm befalls him. But this doesn't mean he remains free from opposition.

Paul could have interpreted God's promise of protection as a lifelong pledge, one that would accompany him throughout the rest of his ministry. Yet the context implies that it's only good while Paul stays in Corinth. Once he leaves, though God will still be with him, the assurance of safety doesn't continue.

Sometimes when God tells us something, it's only for a season and not for the rest of our life. God's instructions may change. What he tells us to do in one situation may not apply in another.

Consider the Israelites when they spent forty

years in the desert. God gave them manna to eat, along with specific instructions about how much to pick up, how long it would last, and when to gather it. This provision remained in place only when they were in the desert. Once they left, the manna stopped.

What can we do to make sure we don't hold on to an instruction from God for longer than he intends?

[Discover more about God's provision of manna in Exodus 16:35, Numbers 11:4–9, Joshua 5:12, and John 6:58.]

DAY 29: HOLY SPIRIT POWER
ACTS 19:1 TO ACTS 20:1

When Paul placed his hands on them, the Holy Spirit came on them, and they spoke in tongues and prophesied. (Acts 19:6)

Next Paul heads to Ephesus. He finds a dozen believers there but is shocked that they haven't received the gift of the Holy Spirit. In fact, they don't even know who the Holy Spirit is. Paul probes a little deeper. "What baptism did you receive?"

"John's."

Paul explains that John's baptism is for repentance, preparing the way for Jesus.

Upon hearing this, the disciples want to be baptized in Jesus's name. After they are, Paul places his hands on them, and the Holy Spirit fills them. They speak in tongues and prophesy.

Next, Paul goes to the synagogue to tell his fellow Jews about Jesus, but they refuse to believe. They oppose Paul and speak against Team Jesus. Paul leaves the synagogue, taking the disciples with him. They have daily discussions in Tyrannus's lecture hall. This goes on for two years. Eventually everyone in the area hears about Jesus.

Just as the people sought healing by having Peter's shadow fall on them, God does amazing miracles through Paul too. He touches cloths, such as handkerchiefs and aprons, imparting supernatural power into them. They're taken to the sick, who are healed from their diseases, and those with evil spirits are freed.

Jesus said his followers would do even greater things than he had done once he returned to his Father. We certainly see this in Paul, as well as Peter before him.

In this new thing that God is doing in Jesus's church, we see the Holy Spirit take a central role. Holy Spirit power fills the people. The afflicted receive healing, and evil spirits are exorcised in Jesus's name. The supernatural abounds.

Some Jews invoke the name of Jesus, who Paul talks about, to cast out evil spirits. The seven sons of Sceva try this too. They don't know what they're doing. It's more supernatural power than they can handle. It backfires.

One day the evil spirit doesn't obey them. Instead it talks back. "I know Jesus. And I know Paul. But who do you think you are?" Then the possessed man jumps them and beats all seven brothers. They run away bleeding and naked.

As word of what happened to these brothers spreads, a holy fear fills the people. They revere the name of Jesus. Many believers confess their sins. Some of those involved in sorcery show their repentance by burning all their scrolls.

Demetrius is one of the locals who opposes Paul. Though Demetrius claims this is for religious reasons, it's economic. He stirs up the people and a mob forms. After the city clerk quiets the uprising, Paul encourages the disciples, says goodbye, and leaves town.

The early church moved in supernatural power through the Holy Spirit. What can we apply from that in today's church?

[Discover more about Jesus's promise to his disciples —and us—in John 14:12–14.]

DAY 30: OBEYING THE HOLY SPIRIT
ACTS 20:2–38

"I only know that in every city the Holy Spirit warns me that prison and hardships are facing me." (Acts 20:23)

After traveling around a while, encouraging the disciples, and receiving threats from his Jewish opponents, Paul and his team end up in Troas. He plans to leave the next day, and he wants to make the best use of his time while he's there. He talks to the people, droning on and on until midnight.

Eutychus dozes off and falls out a third-story window. Even an accomplished preacher can some-times put people to sleep. The fall kills Eutychus. It looks like their happy meeting will turn into a funeral. That sure interrupts the service. But not so fast.

Paul runs downstairs and throws himself upon Eutychus. "It's all good," Paul says. "No worries. He's alive!"

Full of joy, everyone scampers back to their third-floor meeting room. Surely no one is as happy as Eutychus, the young man who fell to his death and returned to life. He was dead, but now lives.

Paul resumes speaking. Now he has much more to say. Eutychus is there, but I doubt he sits in the window this time. The believers share a meal, and Paul talks until daybreak. That's one long service.

At sunrise, full of comfort, the people take Eutychus home, as a live person and not as a corpse. It's a good thing Paul was there to resurrect him. Yet had Paul not been there speaking until midnight to begin with, Eutychus wouldn't have fallen to his death. Paul caused the problem, so it's fitting that he resolves it, fixing what he broke.

As the people go home, Paul and his crew leave town. He heads toward Jerusalem, hoping to get there before Pentecost. On the way, he stops in Miletus to talk to the believers there. He reminds them how hard he's worked for Jesus, along with all the trials he faced along the way.

"The Holy Spirit compels me to go to Jerusalem," Paul says. "Though I don't know the details, I do know jail and suffering await me. After today, you'll never see me again."

They say a teary goodbye, but no one tries to talk Paul out of leaving.

Are we willing to obey the Holy Spirit's prompting if we know it will cause us to suffer or even die?

[Discover more about Paul's attitude toward dying in Philippians 1:21 and 2 Timothy 4:6–8.]

DIG DEEPER: PAUL'S TRIPS TO JERUSALEM

When he came to Jerusalem, he tried to join the disciples, but they were all afraid of him, not believing that he really was a disciple. (Acts 9:26)

Paul (sometimes called Saul) seems to make Antioch his home base, launching his three missionary trips from there. Yet he travels to Jerusalem a lot. The book of Acts records six times Paul goes there. In addition, his letter to the church in Galatia describes two Jerusalem trips, while his letters to the churches in Corinth and Rome each indicate one.

From the biblical narrative, we don't know if there are just the six trips mentioned in Acts (with

Paul's letters supplying added details), a total of ten trips, or something in between.

Here's the list of considerations, starting with Paul's six trips mentioned in Acts.

1. On Paul's first trip to Jerusalem after his conversion, Barnabas introduces Paul (aka Saul) to the fearful disciples, who worry his conversion claims are false and he's still out to get them. But because of Barnabas's intervention, the disciples finally accept Paul (Acts 9:26–30).

2. The church in Antioch collects money for the church in Judea (the area around Jerusalem) to deal with a famine prophesied by Agabus. Barnabas and Paul deliver the money (Acts 11:27–30).

3. Paul and Barnabas leave Antioch and go to Jerusalem to discuss whether followers of Jesus must undergo circumcision. The answer is no. Paul and Barnabas lead the delegation back to Antioch to share the church's decision (Acts 15:1–31).

4. Paul visits the church in Jerusalem (Acts 18:22).

5. Paul again visits the church in Jerusalem (Acts 20:22).

6. On Paul's final trip to Jerusalem, he's arrested and eventually sent to Rome as a prisoner. The Bible doesn't record what happens to him after

spending two years in Rome under constant guard. This is the last we hear about Paul in the Bible (Acts 20:16 all the way through to Acts 28:31).

In his letters, Paul mentions four trips to Jerusalem. We don't know where they fit in the timeline or even if they're separate trips or more details about one of the first six. They are:

7. After Paul's conversion, he goes to Jerusalem to meet with Peter (Cephas). He also sees James. We don't know when this occurs, though it doesn't seem to align with any of the six trips mentioned in Acts (Galatians 1:18–24).

8. Paul mentions a second Jerusalem trip in his letter to the church in Galatia. He says it's after fifteen years and that Barnabas goes with him. It's hard to know where this fits into the timeline or if it's added details of a different trip (Galatians 2:1–10).

9 and 10. In two of Paul's letters, he mentions collecting money for the Jerusalem church. While this could be the same journey as mentioned in Acts 11 (trip number 2), the details suggest it's a different visit or even two (Romans 15:25–33 and 1 Corinthians 16:1–4).

What can we learn from Paul's Jerusalem trips relevant to ministry and authority?

[Discover more about the future of Jerusalem in Revelation 3:12, Revelation 21:2, and Revelation 21:10.]

DAY 31: HOLY SPIRIT INSIGHT
ACTS 21:1–36

When we heard this, we and the people there pleaded with Paul not to go up to Jerusalem. (Acts 21:12)

As Paul and his entourage make their way to Jerusalem, the ship they're traveling on docks at Tyre. While the crew unloads, Paul and his friends seek out the disciples there. Through Holy Spirit insight, they urge Paul not to go to Jerusalem.

This contrasts with the instructions the Holy Spirit gave Paul. As Paul had told his friends in Troas, he felt the Holy Spirit compelling him to go to Jerusalem. Once there he would face imprisonment and endure hardship.

In this, a key difference stands between Paul and the people in Tyre. Though Paul feels he must go to Jerusalem, the people in Tyre feel he must not. These insights both come from the Holy Spirit. Despite their opposite perspectives—or perhaps out of respect to Paul—they don't try to dissuade him from going. Once they share what they heard from the Holy Spirit, they accept Paul's decision to move forward regardless of what he will face in Jerusalem.

Seven days later, Paul and his crew resume their voyage. They go to Ptolemais, and the next stop is Caesarea. After they've been in Caesarea a while, Agabus the prophet arrives. Giving a visual demonstration, he takes Paul's belt and ties his own hands and feet with it. "The Holy Spirit told me that the owner of this belt will be likewise bound and handed over to the Gentiles."

In this instance, Agabus has Holy Spirit insight into what will happen to Paul, but there's no hint the Holy Spirit told Agabus that Paul shouldn't go. This contrasts to what the Holy Spirit told the people in Tyre.

Knowing what Paul will face when he arrives in Jerusalem, the believers in Caesarea plead with him not to go. Although the Holy Spirit told Agabus

PETER DEHAAN

what will happen to Paul, it seems the people's own conclusion is that Paul shouldn't go to Jerusalem. But this is from their human perspective, not based on what the Holy Spirit said.

Paul's response to their plea for him to stay away from Jerusalem is straightforward. "No worries. Don't cry. I'm willing to suffer and even die for Jesus."

When they can't talk him out of going, they give up and say, "May God's will be done."

Paul arrives in Jerusalem and is minding his own business when some troublemakers rile up a crowd to near riotous proportions. The Romans arrest Paul and put him in chains. This sends him down a path of imprisonment and hardship, just as the Holy Spirit warned.

How should we react when we hear one thing from God and a trusted friend hears something different?

[Discover more about the Holy Spirit through the writings of Paul in Romans 5:5, Romans 15:13–16, 1 Corinthians 6:19–20, 2 Corinthians 13:14,

Ephesians 1:13, Ephesians 4:30, 1 Thessalonians 1:6, 2 Timothy 1:14, and Titus 3:4–7.]

DAY 32: PAUL RILES UP THE CROWD
ACTS 21:37 TO ACTS 22:22

"Then the Lord said to me, 'Go; I will send you far away to the Gentiles.'" (Acts 22:21)

After arresting Paul, the soldiers carry him away. He asks to speak to their leader. The guy thinks Paul's an Egyptian rebel who leads a terrorist group. Paul sets him straight. "No, I'm a Jew, from Tarsus. Please let me speak to my fellow Jews." The man agrees.

Standing on the steps of the barracks, Paul turns to face the crowd. He motions that he wants to speak. Once they become quiet, he addresses them in Aramaic and not Greek. This gets their attention. They listen with respect.

He tells them his story.

"Though I was born in Tarsus, I was raised here in Jerusalem. I studied under Gamaliel, who I'm sure you know. He thoroughly trained me in the law and our traditions. I was zealous for God, just as you are today.

"I went on a vendetta against the followers of Jesus. I hunted them down, arrested them, and threw them into prison. Whenever possible I brought about their death. After I had done all I could here in Jerusalem, I received permission from the Council to go to Damascus and do the same thing there.

"On my way, a bright light flashed from heaven. I fell and heard a voice, 'Saul, why are you persecuting me.' (Recall that Paul originally went by Saul.)

"I said, 'Who are you?'

"The voice replied, 'I'm Jesus, the one you're persecuting. Now get up. Go into Damascus. Await further instructions.'

"Because of the bright light, I couldn't see. So my friends led me to Damascus.

"Ananias, a devout man and highly respected by the Jews there, came to see me. He restored my sight and told me what God wanted me to do. Then

I was baptized.

"I returned to Jerusalem and went to the temple to pray. I fell into a trance. God spoke to me. 'Leave Jerusalem now. The people here won't believe your testimony. Instead, I will send you to tell the Gentiles.'"

Everything is going well, and the people listen attentively until Paul says that God sent him to the Gentiles. Pandemonium resumes. "Kill him!" the crowd shouts. "He isn't fit to live."

Should Paul have kept this last detail to himself?

When we talk about Jesus, do we sometimes withhold information so that we don't offend people?

[Discover more by reading about when Jesus caused offense in Matthew 15:11–14 and John 6:60–68.]

DIG DEEPER: TRAIN THE NEXT GENERATION

As iron sharpens iron, so one person sharpens another.
(Proverbs 27:17)

In the book of Acts, we see many times when one person comes alongside another to mentor them. In general, a mentor is a wise person, trusted counselor, or teacher who helps another person grow and mature in their life journey. This can be personal or career-focused, and it's usually in a one-on-one relationship. A spiritual mentor can help in these areas too, but they specifically focus on helping others grow in faith and mature in ministry.

Though we may think of a mentor relationship

as a formal agreement, most are informal and change over time. Recall how Barnabas first mentored Saul/Paul, but then, over time, Paul took a lead role in their work.

Consider some of these mentor-mentee relationships, many from the book of Acts. Most of these involve Paul, but not all:

- Barnabas mentors Saul (later known as Paul), Acts 11:25–26.
- Barnabas mentors John Mark, Acts 15:39–40.
- Paul mentors Silas, Acts 15:39–40.
- Paul mentors Timothy, Acts 16:1–5.
- Paul mentors Titus, Galatians 2:1.
- Paul mentors Priscilla and Aquila, Acts 18:1–3.
- Priscilla and Aquila mentor Apollos, Acts 18:24–26.
- Paul mentors Onesimus, Philemon 1:10–11.
- But before all this, Gamaliel mentors Paul, Acts 22:3.

We see implications of more mentoring relationships through the names Paul mentions as he closes many of his letters we find in the Bible. The list is long.

Are we open to have someone mentor us? Who can we mentor?

[Discover more about mentoring in 1 Corinthians 11:1, Philippians 4:9, and 2 Timothy 2:2. Learn more about these individuals and other New Testament characters in *The Friends and Foes of Jesus*.]

DAY 33: THE ADVANTAGES OF CITIZENSHIP

ACTS 22:23–29

The commander himself was alarmed when he realized that he had put Paul, a Roman citizen, in chains. (Acts 22:29)

After Paul says that God would send him to the Gentiles, the people go berserk. They scream and throw dust in the air. The commander needs to get Paul away from the riotous crowd and orders the soldiers to take Paul into the barracks. Once inside and away from the people, the commander tells the men to whip Paul and interrogate him to find out what the fuss is all about.

As the soldiers stretch him out, Paul asks if it's

legal to punish a Roman citizen without a trial. Of course it isn't, and Paul knows it. So does the Centurion. He at once reports this news to the commander, who never thought to check on this important detail.

He goes to Paul and asks, "Are you a Roman citizen?"

"Yes, I am," Paul states.

"I had to pay big bucks for my citizenship," the commander replies.

"I'm a citizen by birth," Paul says.

The soldiers who are about to flog him pull back. They almost broke Roman law by whipping Paul. The commander worries because he ordered a Roman citizen be put in chains. He could get into a lot of trouble for that.

Citizenship has its advantages, and for Paul, it saves him from a beating.

Citizenship results in two classes of people: those who are citizens and those who aren't. The citizens have rights and privileges that noncitizens don't.

Many churches today have a similar concept. It's called membership. And for many of the churches that don't have membership, they have a similar notion that goes by different names. Regardless, membership has its privileges. But it divides the church into two classes. Members have rights and privileges, nonmembers don't.

Though it makes sense for a country to have citizens, it doesn't for churches. Jesus never told us to get members. He told us to make disciples. When it comes to our standing with God, membership doesn't matter, but following Jesus and being his disciple does. In fact, it's the only thing that matters.

Jesus told his disciples to not get excited that evil spirits obeyed them, but instead to celebrate that their names are written in heaven. In similar fashion, John talks about having our names written in the book of life. Those people whose names aren't in the book of life will be thrown into the lake of fire, but those whose names are there will enter heaven.

Being a citizen or a member will mean nothing when we die. The only thing that matters is if our names are on God's list. Having our names written in heaven and in the Lamb's book of life means we'll spend eternity with Jesus.

What does church membership mean to you? More importantly, is your name written in God's records?

[Discover more about having our names written in God's record in Luke 10:20, Hebrews 12:22–24, Revelation 13:8, Revelation 17:8, Revelation 20:15, and Revelation 21:27.]

DAY 34: PAUL DIVIDES THE SANHEDRIN

ACTS 22:30 TO ACTS 23:11

When he said this, a dispute broke out between the Pharisees and the Sadducees, and the assembly was divided. (Acts 23:7)

Even though the commander didn't have Paul beaten, he still wants to find out what the fuss is all about. The next day he releases Paul and orders the Jewish religious leaders, the Sanhedrin, to assemble. He brings Paul before them.

"I've obeyed God with a clear conscience my whole life," Paul tells the religious leaders gathered for the Council.

This irritates the high priest, Ananias. He orders the people next to Paul to slap him.

Paul reacts at once. "God will slap you, you hypocrite. You claim to judge me according to the law, but then you break it by commanding someone to hit me."

Those standing next to Paul admonish him. "You just insulted the high priest."

"I didn't know," Paul says. "The Scriptures say to not speak evil about your leaders."

This is a rough start to the hearing, but Paul's humble response gets things back on track.

Then Paul has an idea. The Council is composed of two religious groups: the Pharisees and Sadducees. Although they both believe in God, they hold conflicting theologies about him. One of the differences is that the Pharisees believe in the resurrection from the dead, while the Sadducees don't.

Paul seeks to divide the Council and win some of them over to his side. "I'm a Pharisee, the son of Pharisees," he says. "I'm on trial today because I believe in the resurrection of the dead."

A theological dispute breaks out among the Council. The Pharisees suddenly align themselves with Paul because he believes in the resurrection of the dead. However, the Sadducees are now more convinced than ever that Paul deserves punishment.

"We find no fault with this man," the Pharisees say. "What if he did hear from God?"

The debate escalates into an uproar. The dispute becomes violent. The commander fears the agitated crowd will tear Paul in half. He orders his soldiers to take Paul by force and carry him back to the barracks.

Though Paul did not address the reason for the inquiry, he did skillfully divide the Council and avoid punishment. We don't know if this is a strategic decision on Paul's part or if the Holy Spirit gave him the insight to say those words at that moment.

What we do know is that Jesus promised his followers that when they're arrested and brought to trial before the religious leaders and authorities to not worry what they would say. Instead, the Holy Spirit would give them the right words at that time.

How do we know when we should plan what to say and when we should rely on the Holy Spirit to give us the right words?

[Discover more about Jesus's promise of the Holy Spirit telling us what to say in Matthew 10:19–20, Mark 13:11, and Luke 12:11–12.]

DAY 35: A PLAN TO SILENCE PAUL FOREVER

ACTS 23:12–35

The next morning some Jews formed a conspiracy and bound themselves with an oath not to eat or drink until they had killed Paul. (Acts 23:12)

L et's recap. After his arrest, Paul had a hearing, of sorts, which escalated into a melee that almost tore him in two. In addition, God told Paul to not sweat it, because his plan is for Paul to testify in Rome.

But others have their own plans too.

The next day some Jews conspire to kill Paul. They pledge to not eat or drink until they do. Forty men take this oath.

They go to the religious leaders and tell them of

their intent to silence Paul for good. They ask the Jewish council to request the commander to bring Paul to them for another hearing. Of course, there won't be one. These forty men will ambush Paul and kill him before he arrives.

However, one of the conspirators can't keep his mouth shut. Word of their plan gets out, and Paul's nephew hears about it. He goes to Paul, who asks the Centurion to take his nephew to the commander. The commander acts at once to thwart the Jews' plan to kill Paul. He calls two centurions and sends a huge armed escort to take Paul away from Jerusalem to Governor Felix in Caesarea. They leave that night, before the Council can make their ominous request.

Paul is now safely away from Jerusalem, and the forty men who want to kill him can't get to him. The governor puts Paul in jail, promising to hear his case once his accusers arrive. Though Paul is still behind bars, he is safe from the immediate threat of death.

Now, let's pull back and imagine the story from a supernatural perspective. We already know God plans for Paul to make it safely to Rome and testify there. It's easy to assume that Satan wants a different outcome. He wants Paul dead before he can get to Rome and fulfill God's plan. Perhaps Satan influences these forty ne'er-do-wells to form a pact to kill Paul, or do they act on their own accord? Either way this plays into Satan's plan.

God's intervention to thwart Satan's agenda comes from an unlikely source, Paul's young nephew. Paul's nephew acts with courage when he hears about the plot to kill his uncle. His actions save Paul's life. Had the young man remained quiet, the forty men would have surely silenced Paul, and Satan would have won—at least this time.

One small voice can make a big difference.

Regardless of how large or small our influence, what can we lend our voice to that will make a difference in our world for the kingdom of God?

[Discover more about another boy whose small act made a huge difference in John 6:5–13.]

DAY 36: FELIX'S STRANGE
RELATIONSHIP WITH PAUL

ACTS 24

At the same time [Felix] was hoping that Paul would offer him a bribe, so he sent for him frequently and talked with him. (Acts 24:26)

Five days later, the high priest Ananias, some elders, and their lawyer appear before Felix. Paul's detractors falsely accuse him, and Paul defends himself before the governor. Paul summarizes that the main issue comes down to his belief in the resurrection of the dead.

This time, however, making this distinction doesn't cause a riotous division among Paul's enemies. This time they don't take the bait and argue over the theological issue of resurrection. This time they remain united in their desire to take Paul down.

Felix knows all about the movement started by Jesus's followers, which Luke calls the Way. Felix adjourns the meeting without deciding, waiting for the commander to arrive. He promises to decide the case then. Paul sits in jail, but Felix offers a bit of kindness as Paul waits.

A few days later Felix and his wife, who is Jewish, send for Paul. He tells Felix about his faith in Jesus. Paul also talks about righteousness, self-control, and the coming judgment.

Felix freaks out. He dismisses Paul. "If I have some spare time, I may send for you then." Talking about matters of faith makes Felix squirm. He also hopes that Paul will try to bribe him. Because of this, Felix sends for Paul often and the two talk.

We don't know if Felix's primary motivation to see Paul is faith or money. What we do know is that this goes on for two years. Felix never decides to follow Jesus, and Paul never offers a bribe.

When it's time for Felix to move on, he leaves Paul to languish in prison. He does this to earn some goodwill from the Jews who oppose Paul.

People can decide to follow Jesus anytime. But

not deciding today is the same as saying "no." We never hear of Felix again in the Bible, so we don't know if he ever did say "yes" to Jesus. I hope he did, but I fear he didn't.

Have you said "yes" to following Jesus? What other good things can we say "yes" to today?

[Discover more about saying "yes" to Jesus today in Luke 23:42–43, 2 Corinthians 6:2, and Hebrews 3:12–13.]

DIG DEEPER: NAMES FOR JESUS'S FOLLOWERS

Jesus answered, "I am the way and the truth and the life."
(John 14:6)

Four times Luke uses the phrase *the Way* to refer to Jesus's followers (Acts 9:2, Acts 19:9, Acts 24:14, and Acts 24:22). No other New Testament writer uses this label. The origin of this may come from Jesus's own words when he says, "I'm the way, the truth, and the life."

Luke also uses the word *sect* to refer to Jesus's followers (Acts 24:14 and Acts 28:21–22). This comes from the Jews in Rome. The implication is that they see the followers of Jesus as one part of

Judaism, a sect just like the sect of the Pharisees and the sect of the Sadducees.

A third word is *Christian*. Though common today, it only appears three times in the New Testament text (disregarding the times publishers later added it in subheadings.) Luke says the label *Christian* first occurred in Antioch. He uses it twice in the book of Acts (Acts 11:26 and Acts 26:28), and Peter uses it once in his first letter (1 Peter 4:16).

Three more common labels are *disciples*, *believers*, and *brothers and sisters*.

Luke uses *disciples* twenty-three times, but none of the other New Testament writers who follow him use it.

Luke uses *believers* twenty-eight times in the book of Acts. Other writers—Paul, Peter, and John—use it twenty-one times, collectively.

Last, Luke uses the more endearing label of *brothers and sisters* to refer to Jesus's followers. Luke uses it eleven times, but Paul uses it over one hundred. James, Peter, and John also use this engaging phrase.

What label do you prefer?

[Discover more about following Jesus in Matthew 7:13 and Luke 13:24–30.]

DAY 37: PAUL'S LEGAL GAMBIT
ACTS 25:1–12

They requested Festus, as a favor to them, to have Paul transferred to Jerusalem, for they were preparing an ambush to kill him along the way. (Acts 25:3)

P aul sits in the Caesarean prison for two years. It's been that long since God promised Paul that he would make it to Rome to tell the people there about Jesus. Paul may wonder if God changed his mind. Or Paul may question if he heard God correctly. Two years is a long time to wait. Of course, two years is nothing compared to how long Abraham waited to have the son God promised him.

Felix is now gone, having never received a bribe

from Paul and having never decided to follow Jesus. Festus replaces Felix as governor. With a new person in power, the Jewish leaders try afresh to do away with Paul. They petition Festus to return Paul to Jerusalem for trial.

It's been two years since the forty men conspired to do away with Paul, pledging to fast until they killed him. Though they had to break their fast in shame for having failed their mission, I'm sure they're still anxious to follow through. Killing Paul is a way for them to save face from their earlier failure. They'll murder Paul as he's transported from Caesarea to Jerusalem.

But Festus sees no reason to send Paul to Jerusalem. He promises to hold a hearing when he's back in Caesarea. "You come with me," he says. "If Paul's done anything wrong, we'll deal with it there."

Festus convenes the hearing, Paul's brought in, and the Jewish leaders accuse him of outrageous things they can't prove. Paul denies their charges, insisting he's innocent.

Unaware of the Jews' plan to kill Paul, Festus sees what seems to be a clever solution. He asks Paul if he's willing to go to Jerusalem and stand trial there. Paul's not. That won't get him to Rome, and he doubts he'll ever make it to Jerusalem alive.

"I'm a Roman citizen. I want to be tried right here in a Roman court," Paul says. Then he tells Festus, "You know very well that I'm not guilty." Since Festus doesn't deny Paul's claim, he implies he knows Paul is innocent.

Then Paul has an idea. He appeals his case to Caesar, a right he has as a Roman citizen. Again, we don't know if this is the Holy Spirit giving Paul the words to say during his hearing or not, but regardless, this begins the events that will finally get Paul to Rome, just as God promised.

How long are we willing to wait for God to do what he promised?

[Discover more about Abraham's faith to patiently wait for God's timing in Romans 4:18–22 and Hebrews 6:14–15, as well as Galatians 3:6–9 and James 2:23–24, which both quote Genesis 15:6.]

DAY 38: TESTIFYING OF JESUS
ACTS 25:13 TO ACTS 26:32

Then Agrippa said to Paul, "Do you think that in such a short time you can persuade me to be a Christian?" (Acts 26:28)

P aul has appealed his case to Caesar. This will get him to Rome, just as God promised. But Governor Festus can't understand Paul's situation and doesn't know what charges to list. It seems foolish to send Paul to appear before Caesar without stating the reason for his imprisonment or what issue Caesar needs to decide.

Festus discusses the situation with King Agrippa and Bernice. Together they agree to hear what Paul has to say. With great pomp and before a prominent audience, Festus brings Paul in. Agrippa invites Paul to make his defense.

But Paul doesn't present his case to Agrippa and the rest of the court. Instead, he shares his testimony. He doesn't mention why he's in jail or why the Jewish leaders want him dead, though he does say, "I'm on trial because I believe God's promise to our ancestors has been fulfilled." Paul talks about his training, his faith, and his conversion. Paul says he teaches what the prophets said would happen, that the savior would die and rise from the dead— for both Jews and Gentiles.

At this point Festus can't contain himself. "Paul, you're insane! You've gone crazy over your intense studies."

Paul assures Festus that he's sane. Then Paul turns his attention to Agrippa, asking him what he believes.

Agrippa doesn't answer. Instead, he asks a question, "Do you expect me to become a Christian in such short order?"

Yes, Paul does, along with everyone else who's hearing him in the court. Instead of defending himself, that's why he talked about Jesus.

Agrippa, Festus, and Bernice stand to leave.

They discuss Paul's situation and agree that he's done nothing to deserve jail time or death. Then Agrippa says to Festus, "We could let him go, had he not appealed his case to Caesar."

Yet Paul's appeal to Caesar preempted his extradition to Jerusalem and facing death while on route. That request saved his life then, but now, a few days later, this same appeal prevents his release. However, it also keeps his path moving toward Rome, just as God promised.

Agrippa, Festus, and Felix (who we covered in "37: Paul's Legal Gambit") all react differently to Paul's message about Jesus.

Felix is intrigued enough to keep talking to Paul about matters of faith, though he's unwilling to decide.

Festus can't grasp what Paul's saying and thinks he's crazy.

Agrippa understands Paul's message and may even be under a bit of Holy Spirit conviction. He might think about becoming a Christian, but he doesn't.

When Paul tells people about Jesus, many of them decide to follow him. In this instance, no one does. People receive the same message of God's good news in different ways. Some say "yes," others say "no," and some put off deciding.

Are we putting off any important spiritual decisions? Can we make them today?

[Discover more about not putting things off in Psalm 95:7–8, Proverbs 6:4–5, and Hebrews 3:7–8.]

DIG DEEPER: THE SUPERNATURAL EMPOWERS THE CHURCH

"I am going to send you what my Father has promised; but stay in the city until you have been clothed with power from on high." (Luke 24:49)

G od the Father is the star of the Old Testament, which looks to the arrival of Jesus. Jesus is the star of the Gospels, which looks to the arrival of the Holy Spirit. The Holy Spirit is the star of Acts. Luke mentions the work of the Holy Spirit or Spirit, along with other supernatural events, over eighty times in Acts. We've already covered some of these passages. Here is the complete list:

- Jesus gives instructions through the Holy Spirit, Acts 1:1–2.
- God promises Holy Spirit baptism, Acts 1:5.
- Jesus's followers will receive Holy Spirit power to witness, Acts 1:8.
- God controls the outcome of the dice toss to reveal the next disciple, Acts 1:24–26.
- At Pentecost the Holy Spirit fills everyone, and they speak in other languages, Acts 2:1–4.
- Peter quotes Joel who said God will pour out his Spirit on all people. They'll prophesy, see visions, and dream dreams, Acts 2:17–19, quoting Joel 2:28–32.
- Peter says to be baptized and receive the gift of the Holy Spirit, Acts 2:38.
- The apostles perform wondrous acts and miraculous signs, Acts 2:43.
- Peter heals a lame man, Acts 3:6–8.
- Complete healing occurs in Jesus's name, Acts 3:16.
- Peter speaks with Holy Spirit insight, Acts 4:8–12.

- The Holy Spirit fills everyone, and they speak boldly, Acts 4:31.
- Ananias lies to the Holy Spirit—and then dies, Acts 5:3–6.
- Peter predicts Sapphira's immediate death—she dies, Acts 5:9–10.
- Peter's shadow may heal people when it falls on them, Acts 5:15.
- The sick and those tormented by evil spirits are all healed, Acts 5:16.
- An angel frees Peter from jail, Acts 5:19–20.
- God gives the Holy Spirit to those who obey him, Acts 5:32.
- The first deacons are full of the Spirit and wisdom, Acts 6:3.
- Stephen is full of faith and of the Holy Spirit, Acts 6:5.
- Stephen does great wonders and miraculous signs among the people, Acts 6:8.
- Stephen accuses the Jews of resisting the Holy Spirit, Acts 7:51.
- Stephen, full of the Holy Spirit, sees heaven, God's glory, and Jesus, Acts 7:55–56.

- Philip exorcises demons and heals the lame and paralyzed, Acts 8:7.
- Peter and John place their hands on people, who then receive the Holy Spirit, Acts 8:15–19.
- God speaks to Philip through an angel, Acts 8:26.
- The Spirit tells Philip what to do, Acts 8:29.
- The Spirit of the Lord whisks Philip away and brings him to another place, Acts 8:39.
- God speaks audibly to Paul, Acts 9:4 and Acts 26:14–18.
- God speaks to Ananias in a vision (this is not the Ananias who was married to Sapphira and struck dead for lying to the Holy Spirit), Acts 9:10–11.
- The Lord tells Ananias what to do, Acts 9:15.
- Ananias goes to Saul (later known as Paul) so he can see again and receive the infilling of the Holy Spirit, Acts 9:17–18 and Acts 22:13.
- The Holy Spirit encourages the church and it grows, Acts 9:31.

- Peter heals paralyzed Aeneas, Acts 9:34.
- Peter raises Tabitha from the dead, Acts 9:40.
- Cornelius has a vision where an angel of God instructs him, Acts 10:3–5.
- Peter has a vision (trance), Acts 10:10 and Acts 11:5.
- God audibly speaks to Peter through a vision, Acts 10:13–15 and Acts 11:7–9.
- The Spirit tells Peter what is about to happen and what to do, Acts 10:19–20.
- God gives Paul insight about ministering to Gentiles, Acts 10:28 and Acts 10:34–35.
- The Holy Spirit comes on all who hear Peter's message, Acts 10:44–45.
- People speak in tongues, Acts 10:46 and Acts 11:15–16.
- Gentiles receive the Holy Spirit, Acts 10:47.
- God's Spirit tells Peter what to do, Acts 11:12.
- Barnabas is full of the Holy Spirit and faith, Acts 11:24.
- Through the Spirit, Agabus predicts a severe famine, Acts 11:28.

- God's angel rescues Peter and escorts him out of jail, Acts 12:7–9.
- An angel strikes Herod down and he dies, Acts 12:23.
- During worship and fasting, the Holy Spirit speaks to the church, Acts 13:2.
- The Holy Spirit sends out Barnabas and Saul, Acts 13:4.
- Paul/Saul, filled with the Holy Spirit, proclaims that Elymas will go blind—he does, Acts 13:9–11.
- The disciples are full of joy and the Holy Spirit, Acts 13:52.
- God confirms Paul and Barnabas's message by enabling them to do miraculous signs and wonders, Acts 14:3.
- Paul heals a lame man, Acts 14:9–10.
- God gives the Holy Spirit to the Gentiles, Acts 15:8.
- God does miraculous signs and wonders through Barnabas and Paul, Acts 15:12.
- The Holy Spirit guides the church in dealing with a theological issue, Acts 15:28–29.

- The Holy Spirit stops Paul from going to certain areas, Acts 16:6–7.
- Paul has a vision from God, Acts 16:9–10.
- Paul casts out a fortune-telling spirit, Acts 16:18.
- God causes all the prisoners' chains to fall off (he may cause the earthquake too), Acts 16:26.
- God encourages Paul in a vision, Acts 18:9.
- Apollos speaks with great fervor in the Spirit, Acts 18:25.
- Paul asks if the believers received the Holy Spirit, Acts 19:2.
- When Paul places his hands on the people, the Holy Spirit comes on them, and they speak in tongues and prophesy, Acts 19:6.
- God does extraordinary miracles through Paul. Even handkerchiefs and aprons that he touches have the power to cure the sick and exorcise evil spirits, Acts 19:11–12.
- Paul raises Eutychus from the dead, Acts 20:9–10.

- The Spirit compels Paul to go to Jerusalem, warning that he will face prison and hardships, Acts 20:22–23.
- The Holy Spirit makes some people overseers in Ephesus, Acts 20:28.
- Through the Spirit, the people of Tyre urge Paul not to go to Jerusalem, Acts 21:4.
- Philip's four unmarried daughters prophesy, Acts 21:8–9.
- Agabus prophesies Paul's future, Acts 21:10–11.
- Paul shares how the Lord spoke to him in a trance, Acts 22:17–18.
- The Lord encourages Paul, Acts 23:11.
- Paul obeys his vision from heaven, Acts 26:19.
- Paul accurately foretells the future of the crew and the ship, Acts 27:9–10.
- An angel of God tells Paul what will happen, Acts 27:22–26.
- Paul affirms that the Holy Spirit spoke truth to Isaiah, Acts 28:25–26.
- Paul heals a man with dysentery, Acts 28:8.
- Paul heals the sick, Acts 28:9.

How does the supernatural hand of God and the Holy Spirit work in us and through us today? What about our church?

[Discover more about Jesus's instruction to wait for the gift of the Holy Spirit in Acts 1:4. Learn more about miracles in 2 Corinthians 12:12, Galatians 3:5, and Hebrews 2:4.]

DAY 39: SHIPWRECKED BUT SAFE

ACTS 27:1 TO ACTS 28:10

Paul went in to see him and, after prayer, placed his hands on him and healed him. (Acts 28:8)

At last Paul is on his way to Rome. Though he may have expected to go there as a free man and not as a prisoner, he's headed there, nonetheless. What's more, he doesn't have to plan for this trip or pay for it. The Roman government handles all the details and costs.

Interestingly, this is one of the passages in Acts where Luke reverts to a first-person point of view, using the word *we*. This means that at least Luke is with Paul. Others may go with him too. We can assume Paul's companions travel as free people and not prisoners. This means they must pay their own way, while Paul goes for free. Regardless, Paul isn't alone. At least Luke is with him and there may be others too.

The trip to Rome is mostly by ship and marks Paul's fourth journey. Though some call this a missionary trip, a more correct understanding is that it's a prisoner transfer. Even so, Paul still uses this trip to advance the kingdom of God. We also see the Holy Spirit and supernatural power at work to get him safely to Rome.

First, Paul advises that the ship not push forward and sail into the winter months. He predicts shipwreck, loss of cargo, and personal danger if they continue sailing. Though this may be on his own accord, it also could be Holy Spirit insight. Regardless, they ignore Paul's warning and set sail, ending up in a major, life-threatening storm.

Paul gives them an I-told-you-so reprimand. Even so, he's able to give them hope too. God told him that despite their dismal situation, he will make it to Rome and everyone on board will survive.

They do throw the cargo overboard. Though the boat doesn't capsize, they run aground. However, everyone lives, just as God promised Paul.

They land on the island of Malta. As Paul gathers sticks to feed the fire on the beach, a poisonous snake shoots out and sinks its fangs into Paul's hand. He shakes off the snake as if it's no big deal. Everyone expects Paul to die from a fatal snakebite. He doesn't. It's not God's plan for Paul to die on Malta, but to make it to Rome. Once again God protects Paul.

Paul also heals a man of dysentery. Then other sick people flock to him for healing. God is at work through Paul. Though this isn't a missionary journey, Paul makes the most of his situation, and his actions are missional.

What can we do to make our life missional for God? What can we do to heal the sick?

[Discover more about Jesus's command to heal the sick in Matthew 10:8, Luke 9:2, and Luke 10:9.]

DAY 40: PAUL REACHES ROME AS PROMISED

ACTS 28:11–30

For two whole years Paul stayed there in his own rented house and welcomed all who came to see him. (Acts 28:30)

Three months after the shipwreck, when it's safe to sail again, Paul and his group resume their trip and sail for Rome. The ship makes stops along the way, including Puteoli, where they stay for a week and spend time with the believers there. Then it's off to Rome. The brothers and sisters in Rome hear of Paul's arrival and meet him. Their presence encourages him, and he thanks God for it. Usually it's Paul who encourages others in their faith, but now it's Paul who receives the encouragement. Sometimes we give and sometimes we need to receive. Paul knows how to do both.

In Rome, Paul isn't jailed. He's allowed to live on his own, albeit under constant guard. After settling in, he calls for the Jewish leaders. Assuming they've heard rumors about him, he explains his situation, defends his actions, and tells them about his belief in the promised Messiah.

Curious, they want to hear more. At the appointed time and day, many people come to hear what Paul has to say. He tells about the kingdom of God and Jesus, urging them to follow Jesus. Some are convinced, but not everyone.

After the Jews argue among themselves about what Paul had said, he leaves them with a stirring rebuke from the prophet Isaiah: "They will hear but not understand. They will see but not comprehend. Their hearts are hard. They cannot turn to God for him to heal them."

But this offer of salvation isn't just for Jews. It's also available to Gentiles. "And they will accept it," Paul says.

For two years, Paul lives in Rome at his own expense. He welcomes all who visit him. We can read more about Paul in the letters he sent to various churches and individuals, but this is the last that we hear of him in the Bible. The biblical narrative of Paul concludes with him telling others about Jesus. He ends well.

What do we need to do to make sure we end our life strong for Jesus?

[Discover more about what might have happened to Paul next and his plans to go to Spain in Romans 15:24 and Romans 15:28.]

DIG DEEPER: LESSONS FOR TODAY'S CHURCH

All Scripture is God-breathed and is useful for teaching, rebuking, correcting and training in righteousness, so that the servant of God may be thoroughly equipped for every good work. (2 Timothy 3:16–17)

H ere are some of the things the church does in the book of Acts:

- They wait for the Holy Spirit, Acts 1:4–5.
- They receive Holy Spirit baptism, Acts 1:5 and 2:38.
- They meet daily, Acts 1:14; 2:46; and 5:42.

- They pray, Acts 1:14, 24; 2:42; 4:24; 6:4, 6; 8:15; and 12:5, 12.
- They select a disciple by throwing dice, Acts 1:24–26.
- They supernaturally speak in other languages, Acts 2:4; 10:46; and 19:6.
- They are filled with the Holy Spirit, Acts 2:4; 4:8, 31; and Acts 9:17.
- They prophesy, Acts 2:17–18; 19:6; and 21:9.
- They enjoy the favor of the people, Acts 2:47 and 5:13.
- They baptize converts, Acts 2:41; 8:12–13, 36–38; 10:47–48; 16:15, 33; 18:8; and 19:5.
- They teach about Jesus, Acts 2:42; 4:2; 5:21, 28, 42; 13:12; and 18:11.
- They share meals, Acts 2:42, 46 and 20:7, 11. (See Dig Deeper: Let's Break Bread, after "4: A Biblical Model for Church.")
- They focus on community, Acts 2:42–47 and 4:32–35.
- They share their resources with each other, Acts 2:45 and 4:32.

- They perform many signs and wonders, Acts 2:43; 4:30; 5:12; 6:8; 14:3; and 15:12.
- They heal people, Acts 3:6–8; 5:16; 8:7; 9:34; 14:8–10; 19:12; and 28:8.
- They tell others about Jesus, which occurs because they first heal people, cast out demons, and perform other supernatural acts, Acts 3:11–12; 8:6; 9:34–35, 40–42; and 13:11–12.
- They can't stop witnessing, Acts 4:20.
- They seek unity and avoid division, Acts 4:32, which Paul instructs in 2 Corinthians 13:11 and Philippians 4:2.
- They balance spiritual needs with physical needs, Acts 6:2.
- They select deacons by approving the slate recommended by the believers, Acts 6:5–6.
- They cast out demons and evil spirits, Acts 8:7 and 19:12.
- Though they experience times of stress, they also have joy, Acts 8:8; 13:52; 14:17; and 16:34.
- Though they experience opposition, they also have peace, Acts 9:31; 10:34–

36; and 15:33, as Paul instructs in
2 Corinthians 13:11.

- They raise people from the dead, Acts
  9:40 and 20:9–10.

- They preach the good news, Acts 5:42;
  8:4, 25, 40; 9:20, 27; 10:42; 14:7, 21, 25;
  15:35–36; 16:10; 17:13; 18:5; 20:20; and
  26:20. (See Dig Deeper: The Eleven
  Sermons in the book of Acts, after "11:
  Stephen's Sermon.")

- They worship and praise God, Acts
  11:18; 13:2, 16; 21:20; and 24:11.

- They encourage each other, Acts 11:23;
  15:32; 16:40; 18:27; 20:2; and 27:36, as
  instructed in 2 Corinthians 13:11,
  1 Thessalonians 4:18, 1 Thessalonians
  5:11, and Hebrews 3:13.

- They take a collection for other believers
  in need, but they don't take offerings for
  themselves, Acts 11:29–30, also Romans
  15:26, 1 Corinthians 16:1–2, and
  2 Corinthians 8:19.

- They fast, Acts 13:2.

- They pray and fast, Acts 13:3 and 14:23.

- They commission missionaries to tell

others about Jesus, Acts 13:2–3; 15:3; and 19:22.

- They let the Holy Spirit guide them, Acts 13:2, 4 and 15:28.
- In most cases, they appoint leaders Acts 14:23 and 15:2, also Titus 1:5.
- They deal with false teachers, Acts 15:1–19.
- They make decisions by reaching a consensus guided by the Holy Spirit, not by voting, Acts 15:28.
- They meet in homes and public places, Acts 2:46; 17:17; and 19:9.

But don't forget persecution:

- They spend time in jail for their faith, Acts 4:3; 5:18; 8:3; 12:4–5; 16:23; 20:23; 24:27; and 26:10.
- They face death for their faith, Acts 5:33; 14:5, 19; 20:3, 19; 23:12–13; and 25:3.
- They die for their faith, Acts 7:58–60; 12:2; 22:4; and 26:10.

How can these examples of the early church inform our practices today?

[Discover more about what God thinks about some of his churches in Revelation 2–3.]

Explore how to better align today's church practices with the New Testament narrative in my book *Jesus's Broken Church*.

If you liked *Acts Bible Study*, please leave a review online. Your review will help others discover this book and encourage them to read it too.

Thank you.

BOOKS IN THE 40-DAY BIBLE STUDY SERIES

Which book do you want to read next in the 40-Day Bible Study Series**?**

- Dear Theophilus (the Gospel of **Luke**, formerly That You May Know)
- Dear Theophilus, Isaiah (formerly For Unto Us)
- Dear Theophilus, Minor Prophets (formerly Return to Me)
- Dear Theophilus, Job (formerly I Hope in Him)
- Living Water (**John**)
- Love Is Patient (**1 and 2 Corinthians**)
- Revelation Bible Study (formerly A New Heaven and a New Earth)

- Love One Another (**1, 2, and 3 John**)
- Run with Perseverance (**Hebrews**)
- James and Jude Bible Study
- Matthew Bible Study
- 1 & 2 Peter Bible Study
- Mark Bible Study (available in 2025)

FOR SMALL GROUPS, SUNDAY SCHOOL, AND CLASSES

Acts Bible Study makes an ideal eight-week Bible study discussion guide for small groups, Sunday School, and classes. To prepare for the conversation, read one chapter of this book each weekday, Monday through Friday.

- Week 1: read 1 through 5.
- Week 2: read 6 through 10.
- Week 3: read 11 through 15.
- Week 4: read 16 through 20.
- Week 5: read 21 through 25.
- Week 6: read 26 through 30.
- Week 7: read 31 through 35.
- Week 8: read 36 through 40.

When you get together, discuss the questions at the end of each chapter. The leader can use all the questions to guide your discussion or pick which ones to focus on.

Before you begin, pray as a group. Ask for Holy Spirit insight and clarity.

As you consider each chapter's questions:

- Look for how this can grow your understanding of the Bible.
- Evaluate how this can expand your faith perspective.
- Consider what you need to change in how you live your lives.

End by asking God to help apply what you've learned.

May God bless you as you read and study his Word.

IF YOU'RE NEW TO THE BIBLE

Each entry in this book contains Bible references. These can guide you if you want to learn more. If you're not familiar with the Bible, here's an overview to get you started, give some context, and minimize confusion.

First, the Bible is a collection of works written by various authors over several centuries. Think of the Bible as a diverse anthology of godly communication. It contains historical accounts, poetry, songs, letters of instruction and encouragement, messages from God sent through his representatives, and prophecies.

Most versions of the Bible have sixty-six books grouped into two sections: The Old Testament and the New Testament. The Old Testament contains thirty-nine books that precede and anticipate Jesus. The New Testament includes twenty-seven books and covers Jesus's life and the work of his followers.

The reference notations in the Bible, such as Romans 3:23, are analogous to line numbers in a Shakespearean play. They serve as a study aid. Since the Bible is much longer and more complex than a play, its reference notations are more involved.

As already mentioned, the Bible is an amalgam of books, or sections, such as Genesis, Psalms, or Matthew. These are the names given to them, over time, based on the piece's author, audience, or purpose.

In the 1200s, each book was divided into chapters, such as Acts 2 or Psalm 23. In the 1500s, the chapters were further subdivided into verses, such as John 3:16. Let's use this as an example.

The name of the book (John) appears first, followed by the chapter number (3), a colon, and then the verse number (16). Sometimes called a chapter-verse reference notation, this helps people quickly find a specific text regardless of their version of the Bible.

Although the goal was to place these chapter and verse divisions at logical breaks, they sometimes seem arbitrary. Therefore, it's good practice to read what precedes and follows each passage you're studying. The text before or after it may contain relevant insights into the portion you're exploring.

Here's how to look up a specific passage in the Bible based on its reference: Most Bibles contain a table of contents, which gives the page number for the beginning of each book. Start there. Locate the book you want to read, and turn to that page. Then flip forward to the chapter you want. Last, skim that chapter to locate the specific verse.

If you want to read online, enter the reference into BibleGateway.com or BibleHub.com. Also check out the YouVersion app.

Learn more about the greatest book ever written at ABibleADay.com, which provides a Bible blog, summaries of the books of the Bible, a dictionary of Bible terms, Bible reading plans, and other resources.

ABOUT PETER DEHAAN

Peter DeHaan, PhD, wants to change the world one word at a time. His books and blog posts discuss God, the Bible, and church, geared toward spiritual seekers and church dropouts. Many people feel church has let them down, and Peter seeks to encourage them as they search for a place to belong.

But he's not afraid to ask tough questions or make religious people squirm. He's not trying to be provocative. Instead, he seeks truth, even if it makes people uncomfortable. Peter urges Christians to push past the status quo and reexamine how they practice their faith in every part of their lives.

Peter earned his doctorate, awarded with high distinction, from Trinity College of the Bible and Theological Seminary. He lives with his wife in beautiful Southwest Michigan and wrangles crossword puzzles in his spare time.

A lifelong student of Scripture, Peter wrote the 1,000-page website ABibleADay.com to encourage people to explore the Bible, the greatest book ever written. His popular blog, at PeterDeHaan.com, addresses biblical Christianity to build a faith that matters.

Read his blog, receive his newsletter, and learn more at PeterDeHaan.com.

BOOKS BY PETER DEHAAN

40-Day Bible Study Series

Dear Theophilus (the Gospel of Luke, formerly That You May Know)

Acts Bible Study (formerly Dear Theophilus Acts/Tongues of Fire)

Dear Theophilus, Isaiah (formerly For Unto Us)

Dear Theophilus, Minor Prophets (formerly Return to Me)

Dear Theophilus, Job (formerly I Hope in Him)

Living Water (the Gospel of John)

Love Is Patient (Paul's letters to the Corinthians)

Revelation Bible Study (formerly A New Heaven and a New Earth)

Love One Another (John's letters)

Run with Perseverance (the book of Hebrews)

James and Jude Bible Study

Matthew Bible Study

1 & 2 Peter Bible Study

Mark Bible Study (available in 2025)

Holiday Celebration Series

The Advent of Jesus

The Passion of Jesus (Lent)

The Victory of Jesus (Easter

The Ministry of Jesus

Bible Character Sketches Series

Women of the Bible

The Friends and Foes of Jesus

Old Testament Sinners and Saints

More Old Testament Sinners and Saints

Heroes and Heavies of the Apocrypha

200 Old Testament Sinners and Saints

Visiting Churches Series

52 Churches

The 52 Churches Workbook

More Than 52 Churches

The More Than 52 Churches Workbook

Shopping for Church

Visiting Online Church

Other Books

Elephant God

Jesus's Broken Church

Martin Luther's 95 Theses (formerly *95 Tweets*)

The Christian Church's LGBTQ Failure

Bridging the Sacred-Secular Divide (formerly *Woodpecker Wars*)

Beyond Psalm 150

How Big Is Your Tent?

For the latest list of all Peter's books, go to PeterDeHaan.com/books.